"Peg O'Connor speaks to the heart of the struggles that get in the way of spirituality and recovery, and how to move through them. Her work is important not only for people with addiction but also in helping those who love them find their own recovery and spiritual connection."

— P. Casey Arrillaga, author of *Realistic Hope: The Family Survival Guide for Facing Alcoholism and Other Addictions* and host of "Addiction and the Family" Podcast

"Peg O'Connor brings together the poignant writing of philosopher and psychologist William James and her own deep insights into addiction and recovery in this joyfully readable and timely book. Using James' own case studies as an overall framework, O'Connor vividly describes the depths and shallows that sufferers of addiction may experience, and the many ways in which conversion and change can happen."

— Candice Shelby, author of *Addiction: A Philosophical Perspective*

"Peg O'Connor's *Higher and Friendly Powers* shows the way to freedom from addiction without requiring belief in the God or gods of any sectarian tradition. A brilliant and important book!"

— Owen Flanagan, Professor Emeritus, Duke University

"With a light touch and lucid prose, Peg O'Connor finds in the writings of William James a much-needed corrective to the heavy-handed religiosity that permeates so much understanding of addiction and recovery — in AA and elsewhere — while yet finding room for experiences of suffering, conversion, renunciation, communion, connection, and even faith. Part philosophy and part guide to life, this eclectic and deeply humane book puts the individual psychology of addiction back where it belongs, on center stage."

— Hanna Pickard, Bloomberg Distinguished Professor of Philosophy and Bioethics, Johns Hopkins University

"O'Connor wisely navigates a course between the William James "advocates" in academia and 12 Step "Big book thumpers," each of whom are possessive of their own intellectual history. This book will satisfy both and allow both to learn and grow."

— Paul Schulte, author of *Cravings for Deliverance: How William James, the Father of American Psychology, Inspired Alcoholics Anonymous*

HIGHER
AND
FRIENDLY
POWERS

HIGHER
AND FRIENDLY
POWERS

Transforming Addiction and Suffering

PEG O'CONNOR

Design by Melody Stanford Martin

Published by Wildhouse Publications. No part of this book
may be reproduced in any manner without the written
permission from the publisher, except in brief quotations
embodied in critical articles or reviews. Contact info@wild-
housepublications.com.

Printed in the USA

ISBN 978-1-7360750-6-7

The whole bill against alcohol is its treachery. Its happiness is an illusion and seven other devils return.

— William James, "The Effects of Alcohol"

For my parents, Ann and Jack,
who provided the wind
beneath my wings and the
sneakers on my feet.

Contents

Preface

Intellectual giant of the late 19th and early 20th centuries. Physician. Philosopher. Founder of the academic department of psychology at Harvard University. Quivering mass of fear. Contemplator of suicide. Experimenter with nitrous oxide. Big brother worrying about and cleaning up the messes of his alcoholic brother for decades. Author of *The Varieties of Religious Experience*, a sanity preserving and life saving book for many. Meet William James.

William James knew acute suffering from the inside. As a young man he was wracked with doubt, despair, and dread to the point of seriously contemplating suicide. For roughly five years, he was nearly incapacitated with various nervous disorders, panic, and extreme melancholia. James knew that his suffering was a full-bodied condition; it was impossible to draw the line between mental/psychological suffering and physical suffering. When James reached the point where suicide was a robust option, he understood himself to have made a conscious decision to believe that life was worth living. That belief, he would later argue, helped to bring about the fact for him that life was worth living.

James was also intimately acquainted with the suffering of others and the suffering that comes from not being able to eliminate or even ameliorate their suffering. Members of his family, including his formidable father and four siblings, suffered many of the same nervous disorders and physical ailments. It is his brother, Bob, who perhaps was in his mind as he wrote the lectures that became *Varieties*. For most of his adult life, Bob was caught in a cycle of bad bouts of drinking, stays at "asylums for the inebriate," periods of calm and perhaps abstinence, slips, and full blown relapses. As his closest sibling in terms of relationship and proximity, William lived that cycle with Bob.

We who struggle with addiction and those who love, live, or work with us have a wonderful traveling companion in William James as we navigate the twists and turns of our lives. The big question of life, James might say, is how each of us will accept the universe. Will we do so only in part and grudgingly or wholly and heartily? Will grievance be the key of our lives? We who struggle with addiction confront these questions daily. How will we live their answers? William James can help each of us embrace our own slices of the universe and orient our lives around gratitude instead of grievance.

Acknowledgements

I have referred to this book manuscript as my problem child. It has taken a village to raise it. Without the help of astute readers and supportive family and friends, all this writing would have been a set of unruly and untamed documents on my hard drive that I would dutifully move each time I had to get a new computer. Yes, I know about cloud storage. Instead, here is a book I hope is useful to people wondering about addiction and recovery.

Over the last several years, my brother, John, has challenged and encouraged me to go further and bigger with this book. He is a viable contender for title of My Biggest Fan, though I do think our sainted mother isn't willing to pass on that title yet. Like Queen Elizabeth II, she's tiny but tough.

I owe special thanks to my dear friend and littermate, Owen. His helpful suggestions on an early version of the manuscript helped me to significantly reframe this project. He urged me to trust myself to write the book I wanted to write. How Owen came to suggest Wildhouse Publications seems straight out of fiction involving an island retreat, a storm, and a ferry. I'm glad he was on that boat.

I am fortunate—blessed even—to have caring, whip-smart, wickedly funny friends. They make my wonderful life possible. Whether it is walking dogs, smacking tennis balls, or hanging out in person or on video call, they are a steady and steadying presence in my life. Patty and VB, Joan and David, Amy and Dave, and Lynn my fellow GoGo, I am so grateful. My Friday tennis group has a special place in my heart, so thanks Dee, Eve, Rada, and Billie Jean. Sunday mornings found me on court with Mark, Wes, John, and Art. Susan, I appreciate the conversation that began at the net and happily continues.

I describe my bestie, MB, as the friend who in third grade would jump right into the pig pile for me and only later in detention would ask what was going on. Thanks for jumping, MB. Thanks, Susan, for starting a conversation about pups, poetry, and memoirs at the dog park. I thank Patty for a friendship started with an act of bravery on her part and that I cherish.

Thanks to Polly for coming into my life when it was time to start something new.

Clooney knows he's my heart.

Finally, I am grateful to have had the opportunity to work with Andrea Hollingsworth of Wildhouse Publications. She is an editor extraordinaire.

Note on Sources and Citations

Most of the quotations from William James come from *The Varieties of Religious Experience* unless otherwise noted. *Varieties* is now in the public domain, which means there are multiple editions available. I have used the Oxford Classics Edition published in 2012. Page numbers in the text correspond to that edition. The chapter titles in *Varieties* are descriptive and helpful, so any reader should be able to find these quotations in other editions.

Citations for James's other works appear in the endnotes at the back of the book. Full bibliographic information appears both in the notes and in the bibliography.

I have drawn from several excellent biographies about William James and his family. Information on those texts can also be found both in the endnotes and the bibliography.

Chapter One

Anything Larger Will Do to Take the Next Step

The sense of Presence of a higher and friendly power seems to be the fundamental feature in the spiritual life.

WILLIAM JAMES

He was a hard drinking failed businessman in 1934. Barely surviving the stock market crash, watching his dreams fade away, and living off his in-laws, he had fallen into a deep abyss of depression. He had tried to stop drinking more times than he could count. Utterly desperate, he checked himself in at the Charles B. Towns hospital in New York, whose mission it was to remove the "poison" of alcohol and drugs and any cravings for them from a person. Would this cure work for someone like him who had failed so repeatedly and epically? This was someone who had nearly unbridled confidence in his abilities to do just about anything except this one thing. He freely admitted that he choked on the notion of God or of any being that could somehow save him from himself. His defiance equally matched his desperation, and he called out that if there were a God, let him show himself. Suddenly, his hospital room was filled with a great light and he felt himself to be a free man.

The relief he immediately felt was soon followed by a dread that he was in the grasp of a terrible hallucination. This worry was not unfounded; a standard treatment for alcohol withdrawal was the use of bella donna, which can induce hallucinations. Thankfully, a friend of his who had also stopped drinking gave him perhaps the best gift of his life, which was a copy of William James's *The Varieties of Religious Experiences*, originally published in 1902.

This man was Bill Wilson, who would later go on to found the program Alcoholics Anonymous (AA) and write the book, *Alcoholics Anonymous*, better known as The Big Book. Where Bill Wilson had been riven, he became whole. So profound was the impact of James's book that Bill Wilson and the early members of AA regarded James as a co-founder of AA even though he had died decades earlier.

William James and his great work, *Varieties*, helped to transform one man, and by extension millions more. *Varieties* provided Bill Wilson with a framework for understanding his profound experience as a conversion. More importantly, *Varieties* offered him a stunning portrait of how his life could be different by having had a spiritual experience. *Varieties* offers us contemporary readers both understanding of how we've come to be how and where we are and hope for how our lives could be different when we change our addictive behaviors. While Bill Wilson ascribed his deep changes to a God removing his desire to drink,

James offers multiple ways—varieties—of how people make enormous changes in their lives without any God. James opens an expansive space for being spiritual and living spiritually without assuming any kind of providential God. Each of us may already have the resources within ourselves if only we can identify and harness them. This is what James can help us to do.

Habitual Centers of Personal Energy

Varieties is a gigantic book comprising twenty lectures delivered between 1901 and 1902 about religious or spiritual impulses. Reading it, Bill W. encountered S.H. Hadley who promised to drown himself in a river if his drinking ever reached a certain point. Hadley did reach that point, but was too drunk to walk to the river and instead found himself pounding a bar declaring he'd never drink again. There's Henry Alline, who struggled mightily with drunken carousing and "carnal mirth." James also introduces a college graduate who spent his 20s drinking and wasting his education and other opportunities. James offers these three men as examples of people who undergo remarkable transformations away from addictive substances or behaviors. It's little wonder that Bill Wilson would have been completely fascinated by these examples.

What changes in a person who undergoes such a remarkable transformation? James claims each person has a personal energy that shapes her life. He writes

> Let us hereafter, in speaking of the hot place
> in a man's consciousness, the group of ideas

to which he devotes himself, and from which he works, call it *the habitual center of his personal energy*. It makes a great difference to a man whether one set of his ideas, or another, be the center of his energy; and it makes a great difference, as regards any set of ideas which he may possess, whether they become central or remain peripheral in him. To say that a man is 'converted' means, in these terms, that religious ideas, previously peripheral in his consciousness, now take a central place, and that religious aims form the habitual center of his energy (155).

It is the habitual center of personal energy that is regenerated or redirected. Our center of energy makes us who we are because our actions, attitudes, or orientations in the world spring from that center and return to it. This is part of the reason James claims that those who undergo such an experience or conversion are "twice-born." In some important sense, a person who has such a profound religious experience becomes a new person because her actions, attitudes, and outlook on life change so dramatically.

The language of "habitual center of personal energy," may strike some as too new age-y, but James cashes it out in ways that are familiar and inviting. The issue is really quite simple: what do we orient our lives around? We change as people when our social relations change, whether by pruning some relations or cultivating others. As we acquire or lose material goods, we change as persons. So, too, do we change as our bodies change. As our interests, values, and commitments change, we change. Some interests, concerns, people, and commitments, however, are far more central to who we are and how we are in the world. They may be much harder to change because they are at our core and not easily accessible. Another way to express this is that core beliefs are foundational; they are the bedrock upon which we build everything else. They are the basis for just about everything we do. When any part of them changes, the impact is enormous and can be disorienting. The possibility of change may cause some of us to recommit and dig in more firmly with these core concerns. But those who undergo a spiritual transformation, often loosen their grip on these core beliefs rather than holding them more tightly.

To make this more concrete, let's start with familiar example. Consider a professional athlete in her prime who focuses nearly exclusively on her sport. Many other interests may be seen as distractions that divert her energy and focus from her primary task. She may bracket certain relationships, deny herself even small pleasures, and shun everything that does not move her closer to her goals. But what happens when she gets injured? An important piece of her material self has let her down, if not betrayed her.

An injured athlete or one who retires often experiences a loss of identity. What will become her habitual center of her personal energy? Who is she without her sport? The figure of the athlete who is no longer in the game but lives as if she were strikes many people as sad or pathetic. When someone loses something that has been integral to her identity and she finds or creates nothing in its place, it can seem downright tragic. That person may no longer know how to live; she becomes unable to navigate the world. Perhaps she had a management team that handled all her finances, appearances, and personal matters. She may be especially vulnerable to exploitation because she simply does not know how to do certain things. She's never had to take an interest. The world may start to feel unfamiliar in significant ways. The athlete may need to recalibrate her attitude toward her new life; she can meet the world in different ways. She can understand herself in new and different ways. Or, she may be less able and willing to adjust her attitude and will instead experience the world as hostile. She may develop depression or a more significant form of melancholy that William James referred to as "world sickness."

What is the habitual center of personal energy of an addict? As a person moves from using drugs or engaging in certain behaviors for pleasure to using them abusively and then dependently, there is a shift in behavior and therefore in that person's center of energy. The drug use starts to impair her regular functioning in the world. The psychiatric diagnosis now offered is a Substance Use Disorder (SUD). The criteria of a SUD are helpful here as are James's three examples of Hadley, Alline, and the young college graduate whose experience I discuss in chapter four. Their body may start to break down or betray them. They may no longer tolerate the alcohol or drugs or they crave more. They may no longer experience the effects they desire. A person may begin to fail to meet social and professional demands and as a consequence experience more inter-personal problems. They may begin to isolate from their friends or family or they may change their friendship circle to be with people who drink or use drugs in the same way. They may become intensely irritable and actively cultivate resentments and grievances. They may stop engaging in activities that had been vitally important if they interfere with their drug use. They may be rocketing through their prior list of "I'll never," which shows them that they are failing to meet their own vision of living a good life. They come to recognize the very behaviors they hate the most are the ones governing their life. Guilt and shame become their center of energy; they are the axis around which life turns. Ultimately, they may come to see themself as having no worth or a life not worth living.

It is true that a very high functioning alcoholic, for ex-ample, can have many interests, concerns, and passions, but the drug becomes their center, their north star. It is the sun around which everything else begins to revolve. While they might be successful in their work and have a wonderful partner and family, actions guided by their need to use drugs may cause them to lose it all. At their worst, nothing else exists but their drug of choice. An addict may well recognize all of this and on some level know that their drug use makes things even worse, but yet they continue. Drugs become the habitual centers of our energies though no one ever intends for this to happen. They dominate the "hot spot in a man's consciousness."

James's conception of social selves—what we now more typically call social identities—illuminates the ways in which a person who struggles with addiction may first begin to experience inconsistency between his different social selves. This inconsistency may increase causing more active friction. Finally, these different social selves may begin warring with each other. Most people do operate with something of a hierarchy of social selves. Each person ranks their social selves and attendant obligations. People tend to identify most strongly with the aspects of self they like and that are approved by others. We hold onto certain views of ourselves and become adept at reinterpreting or ignoring any evidence clashing with these views. Being a better spouse may be more important for most people than being a better worker. Being a better parent may be more important than being the most financially secure. Being the generous friend may matter more than being the star athlete. As addiction progresses, the obligations of all these selves will become more difficult to meet.

Many of us will put enormous pressure on ourselves to meet all these obligations. We may think, "I should be able to do all this." We may try to meet them but have disappointing results. As a consequence, we may tell ourselves that a particular relationship, role, or activity just isn't important anymore. Perhaps we lose our ambition to go for the promotion because it will mean less travel time with less opportunity to drink or use. These different selves may start to compete with one another, or some may start to wither away. Less liked or even reviled selves may become more dominant, which is a special form of torment.

When a person realizes she has become exactly what she promised herself she would never be, she may face a choice for which she is unprepared. For example, those who grew up with addicted parents often promise themselves they'll never become their parents. When they realize that is what they've become, they may start to hate themselves even more. Losing key selves and developing new hated ones are causes of great shame. That shame and loss may further accelerate addiction. Those who fail to meet their own expectations and standards for being a good parent, spouse, professional, for example, don't just fail others, though most often they do. They fail themselves or as James might say, wound themselves. Whatever vision of a good life they once had slips away or becomes increasingly remote. The hotspot of a person's consciousness burns less brightly or burns in a way that makes a person unrecognizable to himself.

James understood the ways in which a person becomes unrecognizable to himself and the special torment that brings. James would say a person's "spiritual self" is hardening or the "spiritual impulses" are shrinking. If these impulses can shrink, they can surely expand. In many ways, this dynamic is at the heart of *The Varieties of Religious Experience*. It is hard not to be captivated by a book with chapters titled, "The Sick Soul," "The Divided Self and the Process of Unification," "Conversions," and "Saintliness." Given William James's firsthand experience of the ravages of alcohol use and his intellectual and professional concerns, it is not surprising that several of the conversion stories that James relays and returns to in *Varieties* are those of "reformed drunkards" to use a common expression from the late 19th century. These people are regenerated and rejuvenated.

When we do not recognize ourselves in terms of the choices we've made and the actions we've taken, we are often miserable. This misery is a special agony that may provide an opportunity to change. The dynamic of that change, or to use James's terms, conversion and transformation, is in part a consequence of how miserable a person is. Less miserable people, that is, people who more quickly reach their threshold of bearable misery and suffering but who still possess some optimism, are more susceptible to what James calls a volitional or gradual conversion. A person may realize that she is not being the type of person she wants to be; she is disappointing herself and others and recognizes that she has it within her power to do things differently. She may be experiencing some suffering and as a consequence, a sense of discomfort and disquiet with her life. Many people who use alcohol and drugs or engage in certain behaviors abusively and addictively undergo this sort of transformation. Instead of breaking promises to themselves, they begin to keep some of them. They may begin to change their social network or reach out to others to create new networks. They begin to shift the focus of their energy away from their use, and in the process engage in new behaviors. They begin to make new habits and establish new patterns. Change may start off slowly and gradually, and that is the nature of this sort of conversion. The changes become quite intentional, and people begin to set themselves new goals and have new aspirations. Small changes add up to big changes over time, such that a person becomes, as James says, "twice-born." She becomes a new person in some way because her formerly divided self becomes unified.

Other people who have fallen to the worst depths of misery, melancholy, and torment may experience a more sudden or explosive conversion of the sort Bill Wilson had. Thoroughly depressed and with nothing to lose, Bill Wilson tried one more time at the Towns Hospital. He had good reason to believe he would fail again, since all his past attempts had the same result. Yet this last time was different for him because something had suddenly shifted.

What is absolutely crucial is that a person cultivates new behaviors and actions. These, in large part, make us be who we are and who we can be. This is regeneration and transformation.

Must one always descend into the depths of despair and melancholy as Bill Wilson had before those spiritual impulses ignite? Must acute suffering and grievous loss always be present in order for a person to alter radically the ways she is in the world? Must one suffer to the point of near annihilation before she can surrender? James's answer is a definitive No. Some people burn with spiritual impulses all their lives; these are some of the people we will meet in chapter three. Others experience a gradual or sudden ignition of spiritual passion. There is great variety in spiritual impulses; their ignition will also have great variety. James chronicles all this variety with respect and reverence.

Spiritual Impulses Burn Brightly

James's *Varieties* is a rich compendium of stories and accounts of different religious or spiritual practices from around the world. James gathered many of these stories through voracious reading at a time when he was waging war against himself. He sought an answer to the question whether he should kill himself. These stories left a lasting impression on James and helped him make the choice to continue living. He returned to these same texts thirty years later when writing *Varieties*.

James was an astute observer and student of human nature. For him, religious impulses are a part of our nature. Each of us can learn about our own self by listening to other people's life stories. This is part of the reason James offers so many rich and varied examples of people's religious or spiritual experiences. These stories were his data but, more importantly, his lifeline to understanding how transformation, regeneration, and rejuvenation are possible even for someone like him. Ultimately, James invites his listeners and readers to plumb the depths of their own religious impulses by hearing the stories of a great multitude of others. In their words we may hear our own stories.

For contemporary readers, it might be useful to substitute "spiritual" for "religious." I think James would take this as a friendly amendment, given how freighted the term "religious" has become. It is also a better substitution since Buddhism does not posit the existence of any sort of deity. One can be deeply spiritual and not believe in God or gods especially of the super-human sort. A pretty minimal understanding of spirituality is that there is something else or something More that exists besides each individual; no one is the totality of reality. That "something else," could be another person, energy, laws, ideals such as Beauty or Truth, for example. James actually has an extraordinarily expansive account of what that may be, and it is for each person to decide. One chooses that with which one stands in a solemn relation. What is crucial for James is not the content of one's spiritual beliefs. Rather it is how one experiences them and how one acts because of them. Spiritual beliefs disconnected from actions are like ornamental knobs; they spin without engaging with anything. Religious experiences fundamentally affect how we are in the world; they affect almost everything about us. This is what makes them so fascinating to William James, Bill Wilson, and many others who ponder these sorts of questions.

James was deeply interested in the subjective and personal experiences of religious impulses. Genuine spiritual impulses are never dull habits. James was not interested in people who by mere custom or habit observe religious traditions, since this is somewhat passive. Religious belief that is so easily passed on James considers a "second-hand religious life" (14). To make his case that authentic spiritual impulses burn brightly, James marshaled numerous examples that captured the attention of his listeners and readers because many of them are so far out there. Some of his favorites involve the ecstatic experiences of Christian saints and some of their practices of mortification or extreme asceticism. James focused on these because the extreme cases often show most clearly the underlying psychological processes. James claimed we learn the most about something when we place it under a microscope, and that is what he attempted to do by describing conversions in their most exaggerated form. James' focus on splashy experiences may explain why Bill Wilson put so much trust in *Varieties*.

However—and this is crucial for the purposes of this book—James clearly maintained that ordinary people also regularly undergo significant religious experiences ranging from a vague lack of ease in living to the most terrifying experiences of melancholia. These, I suspect, will be familiar to anyone who has struggled with addiction. The effect of these experiences and the potential for transformation they offer are just as profound as the bigger, splashier religious experiences of bright lights, commanding voices, or mighty winds. Anyone who ponders questions about spirituality opens herself to the possibility of a spiritual transformation or regeneration.

Higher and Friendly Powers

To explore the range of religious impulses, James compiles stories and accounts from many faith traditions. These stories are his sources, his evidence. They are mostly first-person accounts of people describing and reflecting on their own experiences. It is true that James drew most heavily from Christian traditions since they were most familiar to him personally and most ready to hand for an American academic. It is telling that James considered the Transcendental Movement in the United States in the 1830s to be a spiritual movement where there is "not a deity *in concreto*, not a superhuman person, but the immanent divinity in things, the essentially spiritual structure of the universe" (33). This "immanent deity" is one way to understand the higher and friendly powers that James discusses in a later lecture in *Varieties*.

James most certainly offered many examples of people who understood a providential God as higher power causing a conversion or a change to their "habitual center of personal energy." James often prefaced his comments about these examples with something along the lines of "what we Christians call God." James also cited Buddhist, Muslim, and Hindu examples right alongside Christian ones. Another way James addresses the divine is as the something More to which one stands in a solemn relationship. That something More may include moral principles, patriotism, enthusiasm for mankind, or even better versions of ourselves that we strive toward. All of these conceptions of a higher power/the divine/something More are expansive; they open possibilities and connect us to something bigger than our own conscious selves. They enlarge our lives. Each person's higher power, sense of the divine, or something More is unique to her. There are as many higher powers as there are individuals in the world.

A higher power or something More doesn't *do* anything to a person or *make* a person act in a particular way. Rather, each person has to reach out beyond her own small or embattled self and be open to possibility. Henry David Thoreau, whom we'll return to later, experienced connection and communion with nature while walking in the woods at Walden Pond on a misty day. Some feel such connections when appreciating various forms of art. Singing, especially with others, combines voices into harmonies. Jazz improvisation creates something bigger than the notes from individual instruments. These connections, communions, and collaborations open new possibilities.

James offered numerous characterizations of "religious" or "spiritual" in order to be inclusive and not privilege any one particular faith tradition or denomination over another. One way James describes religiousness is "the feelings, acts, experiences of individual men in their solitude, so far as they apprehend themselves to stand in relation to whatever they may consider to be the divine" (32). We need not take "divine" in too narrow a sense. Invoking American Transcendentalist Ralph Waldo Emerson, James claims that Ideals such as Love, Justice, and Temperance are different names for the same Spirit. When we catch even a glimmer of this Spirit, it awakens, reignites, or redirects our orientation in the world. So awakened, people become more susceptible to change.

In different ways, James warns his listeners and readers to check their own assumptions and "over-beliefs." He also brackets his own so as not to put his thumb on the scale.

Over-beliefs are propositions, values, and even world views that an individual holds habitually or without rigorous reflection. Over-beliefs are what enable us to make sense of our experiences and we interpret the world and other people's experiences using our own concepts and preconceptions. They may not themselves have rational grounds but they provide the grounds for our beliefs and values. They are the glasses through which we see the world but which are themselves not seen unless we see a reflection of ourselves. Throughout *Varieties*, James reminds his audience and readers—mostly European and Christian—of just this. One of James's concerns is that over-beliefs may foreclose open-mindedness and incline people to dogmatism.

Only at the very end of *Varieties* did James explicitly addresses his own over-beliefs, giving his view on what a higher power or something More might be and how we humans stand in relation to it. When he expresses his own personal beliefs, he signals this explicitly. His beliefs are his own and work for him; he isn't recommending them for anyone else. This marks a crucial distinction between James and *Varieties* and the founders of Alcoholics Anonymous.

It is entirely understandable and laudable that Bill W. and Dr. Robert Smith, better known in the AA literature as Dr. Bob, and other early founders wanted to create a program to help others achieve sobriety. Bill's experience worked for him; he lived a very different life with respect to his relationship to alcohol as did Dr. Bob. The issue is when an individual's experience along with all their personal over-beliefs undergirds a program for others. Though Bill W. and Dr. Bob were clear the Steps are suggestions, for many people they function more potently than that, even to the point of being doctrine. The Steps suggest turning our lives and wills over to the care of God (even with the proviso "*as we understood Him*"), becoming ready to have God remove our defects of character, asking Him to do so, and praying for knowledge of His will for us and the power to carry it out. Some people will be able to "work the Steps," by finding enough latitude in the "God as we understood Him" qualification. Perhaps some others will be like the atheists and agnostics who appear in the chapter, "We Agnostics," in *Alcoholics Anonymous*. According to that chapter, these atheists and agnostics might pivot and God will come to those who honestly seek Him.

Some people are neither willing nor able to square themselves with a Christian God, which means they will have a difficult time "working the steps" and staying in the fellowship. One's honesty rather than dishonesty may be the reason why one leaves the fellowship. This is truly unfortunate because AA—both the program and many of the people—can be helpful in the right circumstances.

A reminder from James is helpful here. In the postscript to *Varieties*, James writes that the practical needs of religion can be met with one belief:

> Beyond each man and in a fashion continuous with him there exists a larger power which is friendly to him and his ideals. All the facts require is that the power should be both other and larger than our conscious selves. Anything

larger will do, if only large enough to take the
next step (398).

The next step may not be a leap or even a big stride to
immediately overhaul one's life. No, it may be a tiny bit
more willingness to be open to something—to anything—
larger. What kind of step a person may take will depend
on his particular external circumstances and his internal
constitution or character. Different types of people will
take different steps. William James had to discover this for
himself, as I discuss in the next chapter.

About This Book

This book's trajectory follows James's *Varieties* closely.
Some may wonder what a philosopher and psychologist
writing more than 100 years ago about spiritual matters
has to offer a reader today. James is such an astute and
sympathetic chronicler of suffering. In many ways, *Varieties* is a deeply personal book for James. Tear a page of his
writing and it bleeds. The second chapter, "Generations of
Suffering," offers a sketch of William James and his complicated family. To understand James and his professional
interests, one needs to understand the dynamics of his
immediate family. His father was a towering presence in
a family of brilliance and illness. James along with several
members of his family suffered from neurasthenia, which
at the time was a diagnosis of nervousness, anxiety, and
emotional instability. William James had an up close and
personal relationship to alcohol; his brother Bob spent
much of his adult life in and out of "asylums for the ine-

briate." This helps to explain why several of the conversion stories James highlights in *Varieties* are men who struggled in ways very similar to his brother. William himself struggled with extreme melancholy, contemplated suicide, and suffered significant physical ailments.

Chapter three, "The Healthy-minded," focuses on the first of two types of people James identifies. Before exploring his categories of people, I first begin with an examination of James's conception of self. A person's self is complex and complicated, having material, social, and spiritual dimensions that exist in greater or lesser harmony. Persons are biopsychosocial beings, and our suffering—including addiction—can take root in any of these dimensions. Some parts of a person's self may crave to end the suffering while others fight to keep it alive.

James categorizes people by where they fall with respect to their "misery threshold." This threshold marks the limit of suffering a person can withstand as well as their internal harmony or discord. People who are "healthy-minded" live on the sunnier side of their divide and tend to have a low tolerance for emotional pain. Healthy-minded individuals, as James says, have souls with "a sky-blue tint, whose affinities are rather with the flowers and birds and all enchanting innocencies than with dark human passions" (68). They tend to have more united and harmonious selves and more congruence between their inner and outer lives. The healthy-minded tend to say Yes to what life has to offer.

James argues that we are all mixes of healthy-minded and morbid-minded though the proportions vary dramatically between people and even within a person over the course of her lifetime. James is himself an exemplar of this mix changing over time. The healthy-minded serve as a foil for the sick souls. More importantly, they also show how lives are unified when spiritual impulses are at the center of a person's habitual center of energy. These people tend not to require conversions unless fears and anxieties begin to take root.

The opposite of the healthy-minded are the sick souls. Chapter four explores those people who are deeply divided or riven. They not only have inconsistencies or wish for incompatibles but live in a war zone of their own creation. The sickest souls wage wars against themselves. Their different selves are torn between competing needs and wants. They live on the dark side of their misery threshold. They are people who tend to say No to life and inhabit a world of grey gloom. Several of the cases that James uses to describe sick souls are men who are alcoholic or who engage in far too much "carnal mirth."

Sick souls experience emotional pain and suffering that continues to grow dangerously if left unaddressed. James chronicles three different degrees of world sickness, the most serious of which is pathological melancholy. A person with the worst case of pathological melancholy not only sees no value or worth in himself, but understands there is no worth at all to anything. It is a form of nihilism. The concept of "world sickness" is progressive and maps well onto the DSM-5 criteria for a substance use disorder. A person in the worse throes of it inhabits a fatalism and nihilism that contribute to his inability or unwillingness to try to quit. Having a "world sickness" calls into question whether life is worth living.

The subject of chapter five is conversions. Are they natural/psychological processes or theological ones? Sick souls suffering world sickness may experience one of two kinds of conversions. They differ from each other in terms of how they unfold but not in terms of their effects. James identifies the first type as volitional. They tend to happen gradually over time. The second James calls conversions of self-surrender. These seem to be sudden and dramatic much of the sort Bill W. experienced in the Towns Hospital. James's notion "stream of consciousness," plays an important explanatory role in conversions. A converted person is one whose habitual center of personal energy fundamentally changes.

James claims two matters stand out in the mind of a person ready for a conversion; each is necessary to undergo a profound transformation. The first is the wrongness, incompleteness, or inadequacy of how one is living. The second is what James describes as a positive ideal which one longs to compass. The first makes a person say No to certain ways of living while the second creates a more expansive attitude toward oneself and the world. That expansiveness reaches out to the something More. Having positive ideals and the willingness to try to realize them involves saying Yes to life. A person is now able to "reap the fruits of the spiritual tree."

Chapter six, "Surrender and Faith," begins with the question of whether life is worth living. People struggling with addiction may ask that question daily. Or even hourly. In a talk with that question as its title, James wrestled with the question of suicide. To answer the question affirmatively, a person needs to have faith. Faith is akin to a working hypothesis; it is a willingness to live on a maybe. It is a willingness to act when the results are uncertified.

"Surrender" is a concept drawing regular scrutiny and criticism in the context of Alcoholics Anonymous. The criticism argues that surrendering and admitting powerlessness are passive, debilitating, and giving up in defeat. To the contrary, to surrender or renounce is to put down a burden. To renounce is to put down beliefs and attitudes toward something—in this case the use of drugs, alcohol, or certain activities—and to change one's actions. To renounce is to take an active stance toward change.

James advocated a "substitution view" for changing troubling habits. It isn't enough just to say no to something (I can't drink today) because repressive powers are only so strong. Rather, one must substitute a positive behavior or attitude (I don't have to drink today and can instead do all these other things).

Chapter seven focuses on the new or reborn self who can experience the fruits of the spiritual tree. The unification of a previously divided soul has effects in every area of living. It isn't that people simply have a different outlook on life; it is that they act and behave in the world in very different ways from before. While reaping the practical fruits of the spiritual tree makes a person whole, it does not guarantee unabated or absolute happiness. Much about our external worlds may remain the same; what changes is how we are able to respond to those realities. Where before a person zigzagged between mistakes, drama, and repentance, he comes to have more harmony, consistency, and congruence in his life. A person becomes better able to respond to life's challenges in deliberate and responsible ways as opposed to merely reacting. Firmness of character, stability, and equilibrium are some of the practical fruits a converted person may reap. A person may be able to recalibrate his misery threshold and become able to experience a more vibrant emotional palette.

Chapter eight, "Living with the Acute Fever," examines people who have become unified and are living with an acute spiritual fever; spiritual impulses are their habitual center of personal energies. Our needs, wants, self-perceptions, and identities are always in process. What we need in recovery will change over time, which is why we need to remain nimble and flexible. Rigidity may contribute to relapse, which is itself a conversion. Believing there is only one right way to be truly sober is a dangerous conviction. When people are in a full relapse, they become divided anew. There is a shift in their "habitual center of personal energy," back to using.

James's conception of self as in process is helpful in recovery. Our self is always changing, which means our relationship to our self is changing. This has important implications for how to understand self-knowledge and self-forgiveness, perhaps two of the greatest challenges people in recovery face. Those people who live with the acute fever tend to greet the world with gratitude instead of grievance. Each of these is a significant achievement and rightly belong with the other fruits of the spiritual tree.

Given his father's contentious relationship with organized religions, it is no wonder that William James wrestled with his own religious beliefs and spiritual impulses. This is the topic of the first appendix. No one religion is Right or True in any absolute and provable sense. James was a pragmatist, and claimed that truth is made in the course of experience just as health, wealth, and strength can be made. The usefulness or utility resides in what these truths enable us to do. James's claim that "if the hypothesis of God works satisfactorily in the widest sense of the world, it is true," ought not to be read as an endorsement of a Christian God or any monotheistic God. James was a committed pluralist.

The second appendix, "William James and Alcoholics Anonymous," explores some of the ways James was invoked and used in the founding of Alcoholics Anonymous. In many ways, Bill Wilson failed to heed James's warning that people need to check their own religious over-beliefs because not doing so tends to impose uniformity over plurality. This is especially true when the spiritual experiences of one person become the basis for establishing a religion or, in the case of Alcoholics Anonymous, a program of recovery. This runs the risk of one type of experience functioning as a norm and benchmark by which the legitimacy of others' experiences are judged.

The qualifier that Bill Wilson added (God as we understood Him) fails to be as open and inclusive as James himself had been. The assumption of an all-powerful Christian God (what James calls a supernaturalist account) pervades Alcoholics Anonymous. Had Bill Wilson heeded the recommendation James made to his readers and listeners to be cognizant of their own over-beliefs, Alcoholics Anonymous would have been more inclusive, thereby offering help to more struggling addicts.

One of the greatest strengths of Alcoholics Anonymous is people telling their own stories. Our stories help other people to make sense of themselves. We also become more able to make better sense of ourselves. Each of us is an expert on his or her own experience; we do not need to have specialists or professionals interpreting our stories and their meanings. There's a certain democratic flavor to AA, and the same is true of *Varieties*. James never adopted the stance of disinterested observer passing judgment on others. AA functions as what James called "an intellectual republic." The newcomer and the old timer are equally important. The Promises of the Ninth Step are also a significant strength. They offer possibilities and invite people to live on maybes, as James said. People will live these possibilities into actualities, which James called the practical fruits of the spiritual tree. It is with and through other people that we may be able to reap and fully appreciated those practical fruits.

Chapter Two

Generations of Suffering

Knowledge about life is one thing; effective occupation of a
place in life, with its dynamic currents passing through
your being is another.

WILLIAM JAMES

People who struggle with addiction often become accustomed to being a topic of conversation with well-meaning family and friends and, at times, with healthcare and mental health professionals. We're objects of study and subjects of talk shows and television programs. Many of us, including myself, often bristle at people—especially experts—who engage in research, make pronouncements and recommendations, and offer diagnoses but who haven't shared our experiences. They haven't walked a few steps in our shoes, never mind a mile. If a person hasn't struggled in similar ways, can they really understand why and how people begin to struggle with alcohol and other drugs yet continue to use despite tsunamis of bad consequences? Can you treat suffering without knowing it yourself? William James knew acute suffering from the inside.

To catch even a glimmer of what William James has to offer those of us who struggle with addiction and those who love, live, or work with us, it is important to explore the story of how young Willy James became the renowned Professor William James. There are two ways to do this. The first way is through his family, which is why I offer this impressionistic sketch of the James family. I highlight the dynamics, challenges, and events that most surely would have been in his mind as he wrote about the possibility of transforming suffering. The second way to come to know William James is through reading his works. James wove his interests, concerns, fears, worries, and hopes into his publications and lectures so thoroughly that a vivid portrait of him emerges. This is especially true with *The Varieties of Religious Experience*, the primary focus of this book.

A Father's Towering Presence

Born in 1842 to Henry and Mary James, William was the oldest of five children. His brother Henry (Harry) is the famous novelist. His sister, Alice, became a noted diarist posthumously. His other brothers, Garth Wilkinson (Wilkie) and Robertson (Bob) led lives not of intellectual or literary pursuits but of business and later, art. It was Bob who perhaps was in William's mind as he wrote the lectures that became *The Varieties of Religious Experience*.

To understand William James and his interests, one needs to understand his father, Henry, Sr. In one sense, Henry was the sun around which the family revolved. In another, it was his wife, Mary, who was the center of gravity holding the family together. Henry was himself an intellectual who struggled mightily against the strict Presbyterianism of his upbringing. His father, also named William James, was a self-made man. Old William (to distinguish him from his grandson William) had immigrated from Ulster Ireland to upstate New York as a penniless 18-year-old. He was one of the wealthiest men in the United States at the time of his death in 1832. Much of his wealth came from real estate, investment in the Erie Canal, and the sale of alcohol. Old William's attitudes towards alcohol were complicated if not inconsistent: he believed in its sale but most certainly not his son's consumption of it.

Henry James, Sr. was a larger-than-life character who possessed an intensity and charisma that could be equal parts charming, off-putting, and even offensive. His intellectual intensity may have been forged during a horrific time as a teenager when he was confined to his bed for more than two years. He sustained a serious injury trying to extinguish a barn fire. So badly burned was his leg that he first had an amputation below the knee. When the leg later became infected, he had a second amputation above the knee. Confined to his bed and out of regular social traffic with anyone other than his six siblings, his world shrunk. Perhaps this was when Henry started drinking significant quantities of alcohol as an anesthetic for the amputation procedures and later as a regular pain killer. As surely as the pain was physical, it must have been psychological too. When Henry recovered sufficiently to go to college, he chose the theologically liberal Union College. His college career was not a success, but he did study a little bit of law. Henry admitted that he spent far too much time gambling and drinking. Old William was so disappointed in Henry that he cut him out of his will. William also used his will to express his disapproval of and disappointment in some of his other children by reducing their inheritances. Something of the study of law must have stuck with Henry as he and his siblings were able to break their father's will. Henry and his siblings became people of significant means. Liberated from his disapproving father and in possession of large bank account, Henry undertook a course of study at Princeton Theological Seminary, which was Presbyterian. Not surprisingly, Henry became disgruntled and left school for European travels and later officially quit seminary.

Henry's time at Princeton did bring about one very significant benefit in the person of Hugh Walsh, his roommate, and, more importantly, Hugh's sister, Mary. After a period of courtship interrupted by Henry's trips to Europe, the two got married. Mary Walsh James knew about Henry's tendency to seek what we now call "geographic cures" as well his aspirations to become a significant intellectual. She would also have had more than an inkling of his drinking, bouts of depression, and spikes of optimism.

Living in Manhattan those early years of marriage brought Henry one great gift in meeting, befriending, and becoming something of a protégé of Ralph Waldo Emerson. Henry attended one of Emerson's lectures, and was so taken by him and his ideas that he wrote a very long effusive letter. He somehow managed to finagle an invitation to meet Emerson at his hotel. Emerson was a balm on his soul, helping him to see possibilities for a brighter world. Feeling buoyed by his relationship with Emerson and wanting to make his mark on the circle of intellectuals in which he longed to travel, Henry presented lectures at the Stuyvesant Institute, which was regarded as one of the most esteemed venues in the United States. Though wracked with self-doubt and worry, Henry was eager to lecture on the shortcomings of Orthodox Christianity. Henry tended to overestimate his own abilities as he admitted later writing about himself, "When I take a few glasses of wine, I am ready to measure my strategy with Bonaparte, and...to encounter Antony in rival with Cleopatra."[1] Henry's topics were abstract and difficult, which alienated his listeners at the outset. Henry was unable or unwilling to gauge his audience and recalibrate. The lectures were a failure, and this sent Henry into a dramatic tailspin.

As he had done as a student at Princeton, Henry saw travel as the cure to his distress. Now with two children (William 1842 and Harry 1843), Henry decided to move the family to England. The time in England was divided between different homes with the most important being Frogmore Cottage near Windsor Castle. The change from urban London to a bucolic setting seems to have intensified Henry's despondency. Copious amounts of alcohol may have accelerated Henry's deepening despair. One evening after a very heavy meal, Henry felt a panic and fear that merged into an "insane" terror. That terror was like "some damned shape squatting invisible to [him] within the precincts of the room." The terror reduced Henry to a "state of helpless babyhood." Henry described himself as trying to fend off that terror by a sheer force of will. But after an hour, "an ever-growing tempest of doubt, anxiety, and despair" assaulted him.[2] Finally, unable to withstand the despair, he called for Mary. How, exactly, Henry emerged from that particular acute terror isn't clear. When he sought medical help shortly after, the doctor recommended fresh air, hot springs and mineral water treatments. He also prescribed mental and intellectual rest. Alcoholism would not have been regarded as a cause for Henry's problems because it was not yet seen as a medical condition; it was a moral failure.[3]

During Henry's air, water, and intellectual rest cures, he met Sophia Chinchester, who diagnosed Henry's terror event as a vastation, a term theologian Emanuel Swedenborg coined. A vastation is the step or a process through which a person is regenerated, rejuvenated, or reborn. This concept was lifesaving for Henry and would have a similarly powerful impact on son William as a young man. Henry did not stop drinking until seven years later in 1851. By that point, the James family included siblings Wilkie, Bob, and Alice. Henry continued to write scholarly articles on religious matters but he also wrote opinion essays for newspapers. Henry was a polemicist by nature; he loved to push buttons, cross boundaries, and challenge conventions.

Henry's good friend, Dr. Wilkinson (after whom Henry named his son) counseled Henry to stop drinking. For whatever reasons, Henry's thinking about his drinking had started to change. As a product of his time, he believed dipsomania or alcoholism was a moral failure or a sin. Perhaps with the assurance of a physician, Henry came to see alcoholism as an illness. In an editorial piece published in *The New York Tribune*, Henry wrote, "the drunkard never lived who, in the very Sabbath of his delirium, would not give his right hand to be able to drink no more."[4] Henry's self-diagnosis was that he had developed a very bad habit. As he wrote, *"like all habits, its strength lies in a diseased will"* (italics original).[5] Henry stopped drinking hard liquor and spirits, but perhaps never completely stopped drinking beer or wine. There may have been no inconsistency for Henry; beer and wine were not considered "real" alcohol. Two things stand out in Henry's decision to stop drinking. First, Henry's decision may have been the result of what William will later identify in *Varieties* as a gradual conversion. Second, the matter of will figures significantly in William's own vastation and his understanding of how he was able to move through it.

Suffering As the Family Business

Between 1855 and 1860, the James family moved to London, then Geneva, back to London, then on to Paris, Boulogue-sur-Mer, Newport, RI, and back to Geneva again. Finally, the family returned to Newport in 1860. The decisions to move were made by Henry, but executed by Mary. Henry wanted to provide what he understood to be the best possible education for William and Henry, whom he regarded as his intellectual heirs. The educations of

Wilkie, Bob, and Alice were matters of secondary concern. Young William had aspirations to be an artist, and this is what prompted the move to Newport so that he could study with William Morris Hunt. William was a talented artist but, whether due to the expectations of Henry for success and brilliance or his own self-doubts, he eventually left Newport and enrolled in the Lawrence Scientific School at Harvard University in 1861. William remained at Harvard through the Civil War and enrolled in the medical school in 1866.

William, Harry, and Alice all seemed to have suffered from neurasthenia, which in the mid-1800s was understood as a collection of nervous disorders. George Beard, an eminent physician of the time, wrote that neurasthenia is a "large family of functional nervous disorders that are increasingly frequent among the indoor classes of civilized countries." Furthermore, it is those who live in "brain-working" households that may be more susceptible to this condition.[6] It was also thought that neurasthenia was heritable, which explained why it clustered in families. Henry, Sr seemed to have suffered from it much of his life, with its culmination in his vastation of 1844. Wilkie and Bob seemed not to have suffered from it, though they suffered acutely in other ways, which in turn caused great suffering for their family.

Henry Sr. was a man of inconsistencies if not contradictions. He was an advocate of free love and divorce, though he was happily married. He admired and respected his wife but overall had a dim view of women's intellects.

He was an abolitionist who was opposed to William and Henry enlisting in the service in the Civil War. Whether they themselves did not want to enlist or their father strictly forbade it, William and Henry remained in school and traveled. William did interrupt his schooling in 1865 to take a trip to Brazil with famed explorer Louis Agassiz. Upon his return to the United States, William was terribly ill and severely weakened.

Henry Sr., however, did not forbid his younger sons from enlisting in 1863. Since Bob at the age of 16 was too young to enlist, Henry had to give his permission. Whether Henry believed that Wilkie's and Bob's heartier physical constitutions could withstand service is unknown. Wilkie and Bob both became officers in the 54th and 55th Massachusetts regiments, which were primarily Black troops who had voluntarily enlisted. Wilkie was badly injured when the 54th was ordered to launch an assault on Fort Wagner on the coast of Georgia. Wilkie was sent home to Newport to recover from his wounds but not long after returned to his regiment. His return was too swift, and he was sent back home for further recuperation. Wilkie did return to his regiment and was part of the capture of Charleston, South Carolina. He mustered out of the army in 1865.

What we know of Bob's military service comes primarily from the surviving letters Henry Sr. wrote to him. On the basis of these letters, Bob suffered from a tremendous homesickness and worried very much about his own drinking and carousing with women. These behaviors, worries, and regrets remained with Bob throughout his life. Bob wanted to leave his regiment, and Henry worried he would do so. In his own eyes, Bob was a failure as a man. Henry wrote to him on 21 August 1863, noting that he [Bob] was a great object of pride and love. Were he to leave the service and return home, Bob would most likely lose that love and respect. He might also lose self-respect. Henry understood why home would be so appealing, but insisted that Bob must call on his manhood to resist this urge to leave. All that Bob imagined would be right at home were, according to Henry, illusions. In terms of Bob's worries about his behaviors, Henry was just as direct:

> Now you have probably been doing something of late which your conscience disapproves. I don't seek and don't care to know what it is, but I want you to understand one thing, which is, that you probably have a *morbid* conscience on the subject, and should resist it if it becomes tyrannical (italics original).[7]

In the other five remaining letters, Henry Sr. regularly counsels Bob to resist temptations—leaving the army, drinking too much, giving into fear—like a man. These low points, Henry tried to convince Bob, were opportunities to be reborn or regenerated. In a letter from September 1864, Henry tells Bob, "Don't be troubled; you were never so well off as you are now when your opinion of yourself is the lowest."[8] Whether Bob took any comfort in this "opportunity" and "good fortune" is unknown. With the Civil war coming to an end, Bob and Wilkie both considered re-upping. Henry recommended that they remain, despite knowing how absolutely miserable Bob had been in the army. Neither took their father's recommendation.

Like many returning veterans of war, Wilkie and Bob had no immediate employment prospects. Bob's drinking was unabated and perhaps fueled even further by a lack of purpose and direction. His brothers William and Harry were fully immersed in study and travel financed by Henry Sr. He continued to support them well into the 1870s. Sister Alice continued to live at home as well. Wilkie persuaded his father to help fund the purchase of a cotton plantation in Florida with other Northern businessman and black laborers. Bob briefly took a job with a railroad company but wanted to come back to Boston to study architecture. Henry dissuaded him from this pursuit and instead encouraged him to join Wilkie in Florida. The cotton plantation venture was a complete financial bust, and Henry experienced a significant financial loss. Bob and Wilkie each moved to Milwaukee where Bob returned to railroad work.

Times for both Wilkie and Bob were mixed. Each married women who had some financial means of their own. Wilkie started another business with backing from Henry Sr that also went bust. Compounding matters was Wilkie's declining health related to his war injuries. As Bob was planning his wedding, he wanted to leave and return to Boston. This became a pattern Bob followed for the remainder of his life—do one thing while longing to do something else that was completely incompatible. Bob, like Henry Sr., also sought geographic cures. Soon after his wedding, he and his wife, Mary, visited Boston. A letter from Henry Sr. to Harry described his hope for what Mary could do *for* Bob. Henry wrote, "Bob is the most subjective and self-conscious of creatures, sensitive, shy, suspicious, moody, cloudy, rainy, freezing if need be; and his wife is... altogether in her senses, so that her influence over Bob must be to rescue him from his natural tendencies."[9] Henry closes his letter stating that all the family members who met Mary were so hopeful, delighted, and encouraged by Bob's choice in Mary. While letters between Bob and his other family members indicate Bob was relatively happy the first few years of marriage, troubles were not far behind.

Living in a somewhat remote farm purchased by Henry Sr. for Bob and his family, Bob began to experience the same despair and despondency he had in the war. His letters to Henry must have asked theological questions since Henry's responses once again exhort Bob to resist temptations and base actions. William, too, tried to slow Bob's descent towards a crisis. In a letter from 1874, William noted his own struggles had a more philosophical character than theological one. In a reference to his own crisis and recovery in 1870, William wrote to Bob, "I worked through it into the faith in free will."[10] This is a crucial insight from William to Bob that carries through much of James's work especially in *Varieties*. As much as James had read and encountered other first-person accounts of people struggling with alcohol and "carnal mirth," his most direct and sustained experience was of Bob and his struggles. It shouldn't be surprising that the stories of men struggling with alcohol are ones to which James frequently returned.

No matter how much his family supported him emotionally and financially, Bob drank. He left Mary and his son and returned to the Boston area where he committed himself to the Arlington Asylum for Inebriates. In 1882, he stayed with Henry Sr. after the death of his mother, Mary. But Bob could not remain in one place for long. Soon after he left for the Azores intending to stay for one year. He stayed only two weeks and then made a brief stop in Lisbon. From there, he went to England and spent the summer with Harry. When he returned to Boston, he wanted to embark on a career as a commercial artist. But once again, Henry Sr. dissuaded Bob from this path and encouraged him to go back to Milwaukee.

The following year was a tumultuous one for the entire family. Henry Sr. died, which was upsetting enough. His will was a source of great hurt and anger. As his own father had done to him, Henry did to Wilkie; he cut him out of the will. Furthermore, he reduced Bob's share by the cost of the farm he had purchased. All of the siblings except William thought the will should be ignored. William was not his best self at the moment. It was certainly true that Henry had invested and lost heavily in Wilkie's failed business ventures. It was also just as true that Henry Sr. had supported both William and Harry well into adulthood. In some ways, Alice was the most financially secure; their mother had left her own estate solely to her. Harry was the executor of the will and used a combination of cajoling and guilt tripping to get William to agree to give Wilkie his share. Perhaps all of this was simply too much for Bob.

Once again, he left Mary and now his two children in Milwaukee and returned to the Boston area where he took up residence in a boarding house. His goal was to study painting and live as an artist. At this point, many of his financial burdens had been lifted by his inheritance. Bob's drinking, however, accelerated and he was often too incapacitated to attend his classes. In fall of 1883, Bob returned to Milwaukee where Wilkie was dying from kidney disease. Bob's life settled into a pattern of living in Milwaukee, leaving for periods of time, returning to Milwaukee, and spending time in sanitariums for his alcoholism. What we know about Bob and Mary's life together comes from letters between Mary and Bob's Aunt Kate (his mother's sister). What we learn about their lives is painful and familiar to many who love and live with addicts. We learn that Alice, Bob's sister, so dreaded seeing him that other family members wouldn't tell her when he was in the area. It was around this time that Alice moved to England where she remained until her death in 1892. Bob had an affair in 1884 and begged Mary to divorce him, which she refused to do. Aunt Kate had an especially dim view of Bob, writing that even though William thought Bob was doing well and was hopeful for him, "My hopes are few, and his long habits of idleness are much against him. He told Mrs Alice [William's wife] that he never felt better in his life, and felt just like hard work; but alas—how utterly unreliable are his words, and what a gift of fine talk he has."[11] Kate even went so far to say that it would be a blessing if Mary divorced him.

In October 1885, Mary and their children relocated to Concord, MA where Bob had moved. Their lives settled into a rhythm that reflected Bob's bouts of drinking and morbid mindedness. By 1890, Bob and Mary had a good deal of financial security from inheritances from both sides of their families. Bob painted and drew, which had been a lifelong dream of his. He suffered a particularly bad bout of drunkenness in 1897 that prompted him to return to Europe. When he returned to the US in 1898, he was very drunk. Bob committed himself to the Danville Asylum where he resided for the next five years. The last seven years of his life were cycles of bad bouts and fragile calm. Bob died alone of a heart attack on July 3, 1910.

Devastation and Transformation of William James

The late 1860s through the early 1870s found William suffering in his own ways. He had left medical school to study physiology in Germany in 1867. This was an exciting time in medicine as physicians were exploring the relationship between mental states, emotions, and bodily states. What comes first, they asked, the flush and sweating or the feeling of acute embarrassment? For William, these sorts of questions had a particular urgency. As someone suffering from neurasthenia, wracking doubts about his worth and place in the world, and intense melancholia, might there be remedies for him? William moved throughout Europe for nearly two years, returning finally to Cambridge in late 1868. He completed his medical degree in 1869. Finishing his degree brought little sense of achievement or purpose to William. The loss of a close cousin, Minnie, may have been the catalyst to his own acute crisis, which appears in a disguised form in *Varieties*. How long William took to work his way through that crisis isn't exactly clear. His life did improve with his appointment to the Harvard faculty and meeting Alice Gibbens. Though William loved her, he worried obsessively if he was worthy of her love. He felt quite certain he was not. He begged her to leave him and was devastated when she took herself to Canada to see if distance might help him to see matters clearly. Finally, William came to realize marrying Alice was the right thing to do. In many ways, his decision to marry was a conversion. The result was a reborn and rejuvenated William.

William's daily life was typical for an academic at the time—lectures to prepare, college and university policies to challenge, departmental politics to be fought, talks to be written and delivered, and articles to be published. In 1878, he signed a book contract for a work on psychology. The book took more than ten years to write. Finally published in 1890, *Principles of Psychology* was a monumental achievement that remains in print today. In response to its popularity but daunted by its size, the publishers asked James for a shorter version aimed at a wider audience: *Psychology: Briefer Course* was published in 1892. Alice and William had five children together, though their son Hermann died as an infant. Through all of this, James grappled with physical ailments associated with neurasthenia including vision problems, stomach and digestive issues, and exhaustion. As had been prescribed for his father's alcoholism, William sought water and fresh air treatments.

As physically frail as William was on some levels, on others he was robust. He loved long hikes for the physical challenge, mental clarity, and calmness in his soul they provided. In late June/early July 1898, William was staying in a small town near Lake Placid, NY. He spent his days hiking and reading a work by George Fox, who founded the Society of Friends in the 17th century. Fox believed God was an inner light. One day William set off on a hike of Mt. Marcy with an altitude of 5300 feet while carrying a heavy pack. After setting up camp that night with younger friends, he was unable to sleep. In a letter to his wife Alice, William described himself as being "in a state of spiritual alertness of the most vibrant description." Walking into the woods, he wrote, "The streaming moonlight lit up things like a magical checkered play, and it seemed as if the gods of all the nature-mythologies were holding an indescribable meeting in my breast with the mortal gods of the inner life."[12] This experience became crucial for James in framing the Gifford Lectures on natural theology he was scheduled to deliver in two segments between 1899 and 1901. Though spiritually elevated by this experience, the two days of strenuous hiking took a notable toll on William's health, especially his heart. His heart troubles lingered and caused William to delay his Gifford Lectures for more than a year.

James' Gifford Lectures were a resounding success and were immediately published as *The Varieties of Religious Experience*. The success of these lectures may have prompted him to pursue more philosophical questions about the nature and status of truth. His last works were *Pragmatism* and *A Pluralistic Universe*. In *Pragmatism*, James offers a conception of truth that centers on the usefulness of a belief, which intersects with questions about the truth of religious beliefs. James had ended *Varieties* claiming that there is no one set of true religious beliefs. What's more important than the truth of beliefs is their usefulness—what do they enable a person to do. James's book, *A Pluralistic Universe*, is in many ways a sustained response to the philosophical concept of monism, which is the view that the universe is one substance or composed of one substance. A pluralistic conception of the universe involves diversity and multiplicity, which is also a concern issuing from *Varieties*.

From the mid 1880s, William was the closest sibling to Bob both in terms of physical proximity and filial attachment. William's wife, Alice, and Bob were also very close. William and Alice witnessed first-hand Bob's descent in despair and despondency, stints in asylums, and periods of calmer states. Having already lost Wilkie and his sister Alice to early death and having Harry away in England for most of their adult lives must have taken a huge emotional toll on William. In late March 1910, William and Alice went to England to see an ailing Harry. William himself was suffering from an enlarged heart and becoming increasingly frail. Bob died in July, and neither Harry nor William were able to come back for the funeral. William and Alice returned to the United States on August 18. William died eight days later.

William James had never been much of a drinker or smoker. In a lecture to the Harvard Total Abstinence League, William said, "The whole bill against alcohol is its treachery. Its happiness is an illusion and seven other devils return."[13] William saw those devils playing regular visits to Bob as they had done to their father in his younger years. William wrestled with his own devils and perhaps he feared empowering or multiplying them by drinking. William did, however, try nitrous oxide in the early 1870s. Nitrous oxide, or laughing gas, was readily available and the subject of academic and popular curiosity. In 1874, James wrote an anonymous piece for *The Atlantic Monthly* in response to a pamphlet claiming all the central secrets of religion and philosophy would be revealed in a state of nitrous oxide intoxication. Ever the scientist, James concluded that he needed to experience this intoxication firsthand in order to be qualified to respond. As James was high on the laughing gas, he recorded his thoughts and feelings, sensing that all opposites could be reconciled in a synthesis or balance. Intoxicated, he felt that truth was completely open to his view as he connected to something greater and well beyond his own individual consciousness. Much later in his life delivering the Gifford lectures, James reflected on his experience. His belief remained consistent that intoxicants stimulate mystical facilities in humans; they are able to take us outside and beyond our own consciousness. He writes, "Sobriety diminishes, discriminates, and says no; drunkenness expands, unites, and says yes. It is in fact the great exciter of the *Yes* function in man" (italics original 296). After having studied alcoholism as a physician and psychologist and having lived with its toll on Bob, William James was unable to solve the riddle of addiction. He concluded, "the drunken consciousness is but one bit of the mystic consciousness, and our total opinion of it must find its place in our opinion of the larger whole" (296). Though he was not able to solve the riddle, William James in *Varieties* chronicles many other ways to excite that *Yes* function in people.

In many ways, William James accomplished great things, not despite his suffering, but because of it. His own suffering and that of his family members made him attuned to the many ways lives can be destroyed and lives can be transformed. James witnessed that Yes function being snuffed out in himself and in his siblings, especially Bob. William was able to find ways to reignite his own while perhaps Bob's regularly flickered on and off over the course of his life. Like Bob, many of us who struggle see drugs, alcohol, and addictive behaviors as the primary way to stimulate that Yes function.

Chapter Three

The Healthy Minded

*The healthy-minded temperament [is] the temperament which
has a constitutional incapacity for prolonged suffering, and in
which the tendency to see things optimistically is like a water
of crystallization in which the individual's character is set.*

WILLIAM JAMES

One of the many wonderful things about William James's
work is the depth and detail he offers about types of people. Keep in mind that psychology was still in its infancy in
1902 when James delivered these lectures. William James
allegedly said that the first psychology lecture he hears
will be one that he delivers. This is not vanity but merely a
statement about the newness of this field. James makes use
of rich concepts that have largely disappeared as psychology has become more scientized and medicalized. This was
one of James's deepest concerns and regrets about a field
he helped to establish. In becoming a more "legitimate
science," questions about human nature and emotions, for
example, would be framed too narrowly. Concepts like
"melancholy," "despair," "angst," and "anguish" have been
evicted from the contemporary scene. They seem to have

been subsumed under the more clinical terms such as "depression" and "bipolar disorder." The vivid descriptions that James paints of people who are joyous and radiant, and others suffering and in deep emotional distress and turmoil about their worth or place in the world, will resonate with anyone who has struggled with addiction or had experience with recovery. I will use these terms as James does because they capture so fully the lived realities of people who may be open to a spiritual transformation of either the sudden or gradual type that James so carefully chronicles.

James claims there are two broad categories of people in the world. There are those who are "healthy-minded" and those who are "sick souls." These categories are broad, as James himself acknowledges. A person often has a mix of each but the balance of that mixture can change over time. As we'll see, persons are dynamic and always changing, so a shift in the balance between these two elements is expected. Having acknowledged that, James believes that each person has a certain proclivity that inclines her more strongly to one side than the other. This distinction may illuminate why some people may be more vulnerable to addiction. It may also help to explain the different trajectories people may take out of an active addiction and into a new life.

Since I will later discuss how a divided self becomes unified, I owe an explanation of what a self is. How does each of us have a self and what kind of relationship do we have to our own self? This discussion not only helps to explain James's two categories of people but also provides a background for subsequent discussions of conversions and the significant changes they bring about in a person.

Our Material and Social Selves

In *The Principles of Psychology* (hereafter *PP*), William James explores what it means to be a person. Persons have minds that enable us to think and we have bodies that enable us to experience and take in the world. In the course of daily living, most of us do not pay attention to the ways our minds and bodies interact. We merely act. There are times, though, when we do pay attention, especially when one part doesn't seem to be working properly or is misfiring, such as when we want to move our feet but we can't. Other times we may want to stop moving our bodies when we shake, for example, and we cannot do so. Unwanted cravings, for example, show a gap between what the mind wants and what the body wants. The mind may scream, "No!" but a pulse quickening screams, "Yes!" The relationship between our minds and bodies has fascinated philosophers for millennia and now psychologists and neuroscientists share that fascination. William James most surely was fascinated by that relationship. James rejected the view that the mind and body are separable, which is key to understanding addiction and recovery.

James claims that each of us is simultaneously and necessarily an I as a self that knows (Pure Ego) and a Me as self that is known (empirical self). James regards these as different emphases; the I and me are not two different substances interacting in some mysterious way. That would simply replicate the dualism. Rather, they are different dimensions of the same self. The I and the Me are different perspectives but not different things. There's something intuitive about this view. Each of us can scan our thoughts ("this book is boring"), our bodies (back pain), and our feelings (hurt because I wasn't invited to the party). Each of us can make our self or particular parts of our self an object of examination and exploration. I examine me.

James claims the empirical self (the me) comprises three different emphases or perspectives. They are material, social, and spiritual. The material self is perhaps the most obvious. As James notes, the body is the innermost part of the material self. Athletes, for example, identify strongly with their bodies, such that an injury can be utterly devastating to their sense of identity and worth. Furthermore, certain parts of our bodies may seem to be most emblematic of us. A surgeon or ceramicist may see her hands as almost defining of her. James then expands the material self to include a person's clothes. This may be especially true for those who wear uniforms or are in a profession where one must dress for success. Our clothing choices are often expressions of our identities; we express our individuality (*PP* 281).

A person's family is an immediate part of our material selves. People with children often see them as parts or extensions of themselves. Our parents, siblings, and children are so integral to us that when someone dies, we feel as if a part of our selves is no longer. James notes that we feel shame when someone in our family does something shameful. Their shame is our shame. Shame is a full-bodied phenomenon of flushing, having a stomach flip, or having a heart skip a beat. James continues to expand the material self to include our homes because so many meaningful experiences—good or bad—happen there.

Finally, James includes our possessions and property as parts of our material selves. What we create through our own labor gives the greatest feeling of warmth. We so identify with certain possessions such that when we lose them we feel diminished and if they are stolen we feel violated (*PP* 282). Ruining or losing a precious possession, especially because of our own actions, is a significant wound inflicted on one's material self. So, too, is ruining one's ability to work and be productive.

A person's social self is rooted in the recognition she or he receives from others. As a consequence of our social nature, we often seek positive acknowledgment and recognition from others. James claims there is no more awful punishment than to deprive a person of all social notice. When the image others have of us is damaged, we are wounded. It would be devastating if no one turned around when we entered a room, answered when we spoke, or took notice of what we do. Lack of acknowledgment and recognition from others can drive a person to despair.

A person has multiple social selves. James notes, "*a man has as many social selves as there are individuals who recognize him* and carry an image of him in their mind" (*PP* 282; italics original). Each of us acts differently in different groups of people. The calm professional may be the mercurial parent who is a dutiful son who is also an ultra-marathon-er. He is all these social selves simultaneously though other members of those groups may only encounter him in one of these roles. We strongly identify as members of groups. We see ourselves not just as doing certain things such as teaching or writing. Rather, we are teachers and writers; that's how we identify.

Our social selves are also hierarchical, which means that we regard some of our selves as more important, defining, or meaning conferring. One person values being a consummate professional but may not care so much about being a good neighbor, for example. The hierarchy depends on what each person regards as valuable or important. We practice different relations with different groups of people, putting much greater stock in some than in others. We may feel "most ourselves," when others regard us in the ways we desire. This is perhaps most true in a romantic relationship, but it can be true in any sort of relationship. When the right people regard us favorably, we are ebullient. When we lose that regard, we may be utterly devastated (*PP* 282).

A person's social selves can also be contentious and divided. A person can feel pulled between her different social selves. As a private citizen, a police officer may feel great sympathy for protestors but as a law enforcement professional, he must enforce the laws. As James shows, self-identity is multiplex. We simultaneously stand in multiple relations and participate in a diversity of practices, which means that others are acknowledging and recognizing us as individuals and as members of groups. We actively take on and cultivate identities so that others respond to us in ways we desire. Having said that, we often have little control over how others see us.

If we do have as many social selves as people who recognize us, we will not have a seamless self. We experience and navigate the inconsistencies that we encounter across different social identities. Some of these inconsistencies may be harmless (a Shakespeare scholar who also devours trashy murder mysteries), or disorienting (an Evangelical Christian who begins to wonder about her own sexuality), or even life threatening (a person who wants to be a responsible parent but who is addicted to heroin). Some people have social identities that are deeply connected to their addictions. Consider men who identify as "hard drinking men." Part of what it means to be a man—a real man—is to be able to drink others under the table and hold your liquor well. There is mythology around the "tortured artist." For many artists, there is a belief that alcohol and drugs are the motors of the creative process along with the belief that the best artists all use alcohol or drugs. They fear that without alcohol and other drugs, they will have no creativity and productivity.

Our Spiritual Selves

The spiritual self has multiple dimensions as well. As a consequence, our spiritual self is much broader than most tend to think. It includes all our faculties, which comprise our intellectual and emotional abilities taken concretely. Intellectual skills include deliberating, comparing and contrasting, planning, strategizing, and imagining different courses of action and ensuing consequences. Our emotional abilities include feeling moral emotions such as trust, generosity, compassion, and empathy. Our spiritual self, James writes, is the home of our interests and the source of "effort and intention, and the place from which emanate the fiats of the will" (*PP* 285). Our efforts and intentions most surely can be directed in the world. If I see someone doing something I do not understand, my curiosity might prompt me to ask a question. Deciding I want to learn how to do it means I need to direct my attention and effort to learning. Once I learn, I may become interested in learning more and becoming better. On the other hand, I may find my interest wanes and I move on to something else. The spiritual self draws attention to what it is possible to do and positions a person to make a choice about how to act.

Our spiritual selves can also direct our attention inward, as humans are capable of self-reflection. We become able *"to think of ourselves as thinkers"* (italics original *PP* 285) and to pay attention to how we think. Some people need to walk through every step or imagine every possible consequence before acting. Others leap right over all those steps, acting without much thought about consequences. Each of us favors some of our faculties over others in ways that are similar to how each of us prefers some of our social selves over others. The two are connected: particular groups of people learn how to think differently from other groups, and some of these ways are more highly regarded and bring greater reward and acclaim.

Our spiritual selves open us to interests and opportunities. We make choices about what to pursue and where to direct our efforts. Our spiritual selves focus and sharpen our rational capacities, thus orienting us as thinkers. Our spiritual selves shrink or can harden as we settle into views about ourselves that become increasingly difficult to shake. Alcohol and drugs affect our ability to think well and rationally. We may become less able to weigh differences between short term goals (get high) and long term goals (be successful in work). Our emotional palettes can shrink in part because emotions have cognitive content. We may start to view friends as disloyal if they call us out on our alcohol use, for example. We may become quicker to anger and less willing to forgive. We may grow bitter. We lose an openness or elasticity that is an important component to maintaining balance or harmony. The healthiest or most balanced are those who can maintain a more expansive attitude with our spiritual selves.

When people stop caring about hopes, dreams, and goals (in part because they come to believe that people *like them* can never achieve them so why bother), people become indifferent to themselves. Indifference to one's own self is as shrivelled as the spiritual dimension can become.

Thinking and feeling are both social and bodily. A person may feel how hard she is thinking when she squints or clamps her jaw. Thinking is not what happens in the brain, nor is feeling exclusively a matter of the heart. Rather, thinking and feeling are experiences of the entire body. Thinking is not the activity of an immaterial substance. Our thoughts and feelings are dimensions of our material selves. Our stomachs flip when we anticipate the arrival of our beloved. Our hearts race when we get a job offer. Our cheeks flush when are embarrassed in front of the coolest kid in the class. All of this, James would say, shows how the different dimensions of the empirical me—material, social, and spiritual—are not different things but rather different emphases within the same empirical self.

The Pure Ego/The Thinker/the I is perhaps James's most famous and most inexplicable concept. This is the aspect of self we feel most intimately; it belongs to us as nothing else does. It is our sense of personal identity. Pure Ego really is thought, more specifically the thought that the present self and yesterday's self are the same. The sense of sameness comes from a feeling of warmth and intimacy each person has with her own thoughts and thinking (PP 316). Our present thought shares a warmth and familiarity with our past thoughts. James argues for this Pure Ego by metaphor to a herdsman. As the herdsman gathers up sheep and brands them as his own, so too does the Pure Ego gather and brand past thoughts that share the same sense of warmth, intimacy, and familiarity as present thought. Pure Ego is present thought inheriting past thought. A present thought owns a past thought.

Ownership might seem a strange notion here. A better way to put it is that Pure Ego constantly renews and reinvents itself. Pure Ego is always selving; it is less a substance and more a process. Pure Ego is the activity of thinking. The Pure Ego isn't a substance standing behind the empirical self and holding it all together. It is not an unchanging or unchangeable consciousness. Rather, its nature is change. For present purposes, we can leave the Pure Ego to the side and focus instead on the three dimensions of the empirical self.

What has all of this to do with addiction? Several points stand out clearly. The first has to do with the wounds a person suffers when one of her social selves is wounded. Other people most surely can wound us when they don't treat us in ways that recognize important parts of our identities. Perhaps even more devastating is the way that we suffer from self-inflicted wounds when we fail to live up to our own view of ourselves. This will be familiar to many who have struggled with addiction; we look in the mirror and don't recognize ourselves. We may also recognize we've become what we've always feared.

A second insight is that a person's self can become sharply divided to such a degree she will suffer acutely. A divided self is one of the hallmarks of addiction. Bodies start to betray us, we think, because we can no longer tolerate alcohol or drugs. We may also feel betrayed by our own bodies craving the familiar effects even as our spiritual selves mourn the loss of interests, commitments, and relationships that have been central to us. Those who are divided may be more likely to turn to alcohol and drugs as a means to address the effects of their divisions. Addictions may deepen already existing divisions, making it far more difficult to traverse them.

A third insight is that people who have wounded or divided selves often inflict collateral damage on others who stand in relation to them. Our parents, children, friends, and co-workers suffer. Given that these people are parts of our material and social selves, we inflict damage on ourselves as we damage others. That damage to us may not always be obvious or recognizable until much later.

As selves, each of us is always changing or in process, James would say. Put slightly differently, each of us is always selving. In 1890, James was well aware of the recent identification of the phenomenon of multiple personalities. For James, this shows one very extreme instance of the way that the 'I" and the "me" and their relationship are always subject to alteration. Looking forward, not only will this conception of self make sense of the ways that a person may wage war against parts of herself, but it also shows that unification or transformation is very much a consequence of each individual's constitution and situation. What might feel like unification for one person may seem far too divided for another. James's account dispatches the notion that there is really only one normal/right/natural relationship between these different aspects of self.

Meet the Healthy-Minded

Keeping in mind a person has material, social, and spiritual dimensions, pain or misery can be of all these sorts too. How much pain can a person tolerate over a course of time? How much can a person take? All people will feel pain and distress at some points in their lives; it is part of being human. What's at issue is how people respond to misery. The healthy-minded and the sick souls tend to do it very differently from each other.

The healthy-minded, James claims, just cannot tolerate remaining in distress; their natural equilibrium returns them to the brighter side of their misery threshold. They are willing to make changes in their actions and attitudes to alleviate their misery. Though James does not spend as much time exploring the healthy-minded as he does the sick souls, they are interesting to him for several important reasons. The first is that they are so foreign to him; he himself and other members of his family were not of this sort. The healthy-minded are also important because their lives provide a good indication of what it is like to live in the world as a unified or whole person. They already feel whole and connected to something other or bigger than themselves. Their different selves (material, social, and spiritual) are more harmonious. These healthy-minded people, James claims, are not the sort of people who need a conversion or some other way to become unified because they are already whole. They live with ease and peace in the world.

James offers some general characteristics of people who live on the sunnier side of their misery threshold. These people have an innate sense that life is good. Healthy-mindedness is the tendency to see all things as good. Some people will see the goodness or happiness immediately while others may cultivate this orientation in the world. The thought of evil really does not get a toe-hold in their lives. Furthermore, they have an almost constitutional inability to act in wrong or unjust ways. Mostly it never occurs to them to act badly. When it does, they are often shocked and uneasy. James's prime example of healthy-minded-ness is American writer Walt Whitman, whom he describes as an optimist of the highest order. Whitman, according to James, expressed thoughts and sentiments about a more expansive order he experienced in nature, whether sitting in a park or riding the omnibus observing people. His optimism is willful and deliberate; morbid thoughts and darker views of life find no place in his work. James sees Whitman as someone who believes there is both goodness in him and, perhaps more importantly, goodness in the world around him.

Optimism isn't just a feeling or an outlook on life; it is a living attitude. The healthy-minded approach activities and greet the day with optimism. They act with optimism, which in turns provides the grounds for further optimism. Even if things do not turn out as they hoped or expected, all is not lost because tomorrow will bring other opportunities.

Healthy-minded people say "Yes" to life in large part because they perceive a more expansive goodness as part of the fabric of the world. They welcome possibilities and do not view them with suspicion. They most surely do not regard possibilities as vehicles for disappointment and defeat. In saying yes to life, the healthy-minded are willing to take chances and explore paths that may take them to unknown and new places. They have an expansive attitude and are willing to raise their heads, look to the horizon, and greet it with a sense of wonder.

James cites the uniquely American mind-cure movement of the 19th century as an example of a turn towards
optimism away from the darker fire and brimstone of
many Christian denominations. This discussion is important because it begins to highlight the role that fear can play
in dimming the optimism of even the most optimistic,
which may be a step in the direction of the divided self or
sick soul. Drawing from mind-cure writer Horace Fletcher,
James claims that humans have a dual nature that connects
with two spheres of thought. The shallower sphere comprises physical sensations, desires, appetites, and concerns
about ego and reputation. The profound realm comprises
our consciousness and self-awareness in addition to the
subconscious. It is in or through the subconscious that humans connect with something More than their conscious
self. This matters enormously to the kinds of crises and
conversions a sick soul may suffer.

No doubt William James found these healthy-minded
people odd and interesting since they were very different
from him and most of his family. Can a person always be
optimistic? What causes optimism to dim and what happens then? What might drive a person closer to her misery
threshold than she can tolerate? James's answer, informed
by mind cure writer Horace Fletcher, is fear. An example
that uses James's material, social, and spiritual senses of
self helps to illuminate the ways fear can dim optimism.

Imagine Ryan, a nurse who sees their work not simply
as a job but as a vocation. They have a calling to help others and alleviate suffering. When they put on scrubs, they

feel like the person they're meant to be. Their patients and colleagues like and respect them. They're also a parent who does their best to provide all sorts of opportunities for their children so they can flourish. Ryan is a good child to their parents and good sibling to brothers and sisters. Each of these relationships can be demanding and can present competing demands and expectations. There are even more competing demands across these relationships. Ryan is able to strike balances within and between these relationships.

As hard as Ryan works in all areas of their life, their efforts do not guarantee the results they want. There is just so much beyond their control; elderly parents become ill, children mature and start to challenge boundaries, and dynamics change in the workplace. They're torn by the conflicting needs and wants of the people in their life. Their social and material selves (child, parent, spouse, colleague) are all important to them but they just can't meet all the competing demands. When they prioritize their children's needs over their parents' needs, they're a bad child. When a work project keeps them from the school play, they feel like a failure as a parent. As an optimist, however, Ryan is mostly undaunted. They start to spread themself too thin. James worries someone such as Ryan becomes like a machine that "refuses to run at all when the bearings are so hot and the belts so tight" (90). While it might be tempting to label Ryan's condition burn out, there's something even greater at risk.

With bearings too hot and belts too tight, Ryan begins to feel more and more exhausted. Their body aches every day. They don't have the energy to engage their interests anymore, and those interests begin to seem more like luxuries. They feel their spiritual self shrinking; they're losing interest in their hobbies and can't justify putting effort into them. Their optimism might start to dim, which may feel utterly alien to them. Ryan is the sort who will just work harder. In the process, they're more stressed and starting to feel less like themself. Ryan doesn't recognize the tired and angry face in the mirror. Ryan, like millions of others, may look to alcohol, other drugs, or addictive behaviors to soothe, calm, escape, or provide a temporary reprieve from parts of their self and reality. Ryan may dull the edges of their own knives of fear, disappointment, and resentment.

Horace Fletcher, the mind cure writer, would claim fear is an important catalyst in Ryan's changing life. While fear serves important roles for each of us individually and for us as a species collectively, fear can also become a hindrance that seriously weakens a person. The line between legitimate and illegitimate fears becomes porous. It is important to be planful and deliberate about warranted and justified fears. This is an appropriate use of forethought. However, people start to suffer when they start anticipating and planning around fears that are remote, imaginary, or over-blown. Our forethought, Fletcher claims, becomes fear-thought. When fear-thought governs our lives, we are susceptible to high degrees of self-inflicted suffering. The shallower sphere of thoughts, concerns, desires, and physical sensations is conducive to fear growing and even thriving. Fear affects our bodies in a whole host of ways to the point of wreaking havoc. In heightened states of fear, more fear takes root. Fear has a way of widening cracks between social selves and hardening our spiritual selves. This tends to breed more fear, creating a cycle that can be difficult to identify and then transform.

What is the particular flavor of Ryan's fear-thought? They're afraid of others discovering that they aren't what they appear to be—not the dedicated nurse, good parent, and attentive child of elderly parents that they seemed to be. Others will realize that they just can't keep it all together. Ryan is perhaps equally or even more afraid of finding out their own self. Ryan as an "I" is examining and assessing Ryan as the "me." Their self-assessment is already colored by their own fears. Fears are tricksters; they take on a variety of shapes. They are powerful motivators often short-circuiting rational thought and deliberation. This means Ryan may start to take actions that are both unhelpful and counterproductive. Ryan may physically push themself too far and end up incapacitated. What they formerly saw as positive opportunities are now chances to make more mistakes and disappoint more people. Ryan becomes adept at projecting their fears about possible outcomes and then acting as if they are realities. Even optimism becomes a generator of fear. What if they get their hopes up and things do not work out well?

Ryan may be terrified that if others discover that they aren't perfect and can't do it all, they will lose others' respect and begin to see themself as worthless. Ryan decides they should start working harder, longer, and better so that no one, including themself, could reach the conclusion they are a failure. Ryan's spiritual self starts focusing attention on what they imagine others are saying about them. They begin to harbor resentments towards others, which feels foreign to them. Ryan really can't seem to get a handle on their fears and resentments, but they're loathe to admit this to anyone. They hate feeling this way, but they're feeling it more frequently and with greater intensity.

Recovering and Increasing Optimism

Fear presses against Ryan's optimism. How can they restore that optimism that has been central to their life? Fletcher's diagnosis about fear-thought comes with a recommendation common to many writing in the mind-cure movement. Relax, let go, stop assuming so much responsibility that isn't properly yours, and take responsibility for what is yours.

Mind-cure writers recommended that people change their starting points in thinking. Instead of fearing that something bad is going to happen or that you will be exposed as a fraud, begin with a positive thought. Cultivate even a tiny bit of optimism. Fletcher believed that fear and optimism are opposing forces. Where fear reigns, optimism is nearly extinct. Where optimism reigns, fears are kept in appropriate check and fear-thought can't take root. When an optimist starts to understand how fear-thought is governing more of their life, they have the ability to bridle that fear and fend off a full-blown crisis. Overcoming fear-thought may be a gradual process or it may happen suddenly if one finds herself in a situation that forces her to take stock of her life. James identifies the change from fear-thought to optimism as a sunny-sider returning to her natural equilibrium. When Ryan does this, James might tell them, "you will find you not only gain a perfect inward relief, but often also, in addition, the particular goods you thought you were renouncing" (90). Ryan may find great happiness, fun, and worth when they stop working so hard to achieve them.

James shows that someone who is an optimist like Ryan can recover their optimism and become even more actively optimistic. Doing so is, for James, a conversion. Something begins to shift within a person. Drawing once again from Horace Fletcher, James cites an example of one man who becomes more healthy-minded and optimistic through Japanese Buddhism. This man follows a recommendation to actively rid himself of anger and worry (a combination that often produces fear). Like fear, anger and worry have some legitimate roles in life but can cause harm when they play an outsized role. Suffering will always follow. The man began to reason that if he could get rid of anger and worry, were they even necessary? As soon as he begins to recognize he could rid himself of them, they were gone. The power of worry and anger comes from the belief they can never be removed. The man recognized that once he banished these two emotions, other "dwarfing" emotions like irritability and pettiness disappear too. By putting these emotions down, the man is surrendering or renouncing them. This sort of surrender and renunciation may happen as part of a conversion. In this case, an optimistic man converts to an even greater optimism.

The man worried about what might fill the empty space left by these negative emotions. Would he become indifferent? What he discovered is that he felt full of positive energy. In ceasing to worry, he says, "Neither am I wasting any of this precious time formulating an idea of a future existence or a future Heaven. The Heaven I have within myself is as attractive as any that has been promised or that I can imagine; and I am willing to let the growth lead where it will, as long as their brood have no part in misguiding it" (145). This man embodies optimism as a living attitude. He welcomes possibility and growth with optimism. Heaven isn't something Out There or separate from him. To the contrary, he sees the Heaven within himself. This Heaven he has within himself is one way to understand the Higher Power or something More to which he connects. In making and sustaining this connection, he has an expansive self that will say Yes to life's possibilities. In many ways, this man is much like Walt Whitman, who sees the goodness of a more expansive order.

Contemporary scientific research on optimism and gratitude are catching up with Fletcher, Whitman, and James. Having and expressing gratitude and optimism affect a person's material, social, and spiritual selves. Some of the same neurotransmitters that alcohol and other drugs affect, such as dopamine and serotonin, are released when people are grateful and optimistic. Dopamine signals pleasure and reward while serotonin contributes to well-being and a sense of calm and stability. Expressing gratitude affects the medial prefrontal cortex, a part of the brain controlling decision making. Our spiritual selves will see more opportunities for exploration and growth, which may help to create new social selves or rediscover ones we had lost or banished earlier.

The mind-cure movement preaches regeneration by relaxation and letting go. Or at least relaxation after giving "your little private convulsive self a shake" (91). The regeneration in this case is a restoration of priorities and a return to the more profound sphere of thought. The mind-cure movement attracts the healthy-minded because it is largely suggestive. James writes that many humans ask some form of the question, "what shall I do to be clear, right, sound, whole, well?" The answer of the mind-cure movement is, "You *are* well, sound, and clear already, if you did but know it" (90). In coming to know this, a person is able to say Yes to life. Knowing this does not prevent all bad or disappointing things from happening, but it can lessen their severity and aid in responding to them. If the healthy-minded can accept they are "well, sound, and clear already," the sick souls accept the opposite. Grievance and pessimism govern their lives. The world of sick souls may contract and become filled with fear, melancholy, and angst.

Chapter Four

The Sick Souls

[There are] those persons who cannot so swiftly throw off the burden of the consciousness of evil, but are congenitally fated to suffer from its presence.

WILLIAM JAMES

The best introduction to the category of sick souls is the three men, discussed throughout *Varieties*, who struggled with alcohol, nicotine, and other addictive behaviors. James introduces his readers to a young Oxford graduate, S.H. Hadley, and Henry Alline, each of whom was full of self-reproach and recrimination. Each of them had their desires to drink or engage in "carnal mirth" lifted from them in a sudden dramatic way, serving as exemplars of sudden or self-surrender conversions. It is no wonder that their stories would have grabbed hold of Bill Wilson and others who feel the tooth of remorse about their own use.

James recounts the story of a young graduate of Oxford College who was the son of a minister. The young graduate loved to carouse with his friends and would never darken the doorstep of his father's parish. He worked as a journalist and whatever money he earned he spent at the pub. He was often full of regret after a heavy bout of drinking. He was willing to pass his time with whomever would sit and drink with him. He says, "so I lived, sometimes drunk for a week together, and then a terrible repentance, and would not touch a drop for a whole month" (173). He'd wonder why he was wasting his education and life by drinking so much. He always promised himself he'd quit if he survived his latest debilitating hangover. But once he felt better, he was back to his usual ways. As he describes his own experiences, "so it went on for years, but, with the physique of a rhinoceros, I always recovered, and as long as I let drink alone, no man was capable of enjoying life as I was" (174). The young graduate clearly understood how his drinking was making him miserable. He was just as clear about how much better his life was when he wasn't drinking. Even with this knowledge, or perhaps because of the torment of this knowledge, he kept drinking.

James offers an account from a man named Henry Alline who would go on to become a Christian evangelist after his conversion. I quote at length because his language is so evocative:

> I was now very moral in my life, but found no rest of conscience. I began to be esteemed in young company, who knew nothing of my mind all this while, and their esteem began to be a snare for my soul, for soon I began to be fond of carnal mirth, though I still flattered myself that if I did not get drunk, nor curse, nor swear, there would be no sin in frolicking and

carnal mirth, and I thought God would indulge young people with some (what I called simple or civil) recreation...When I was distressed by or threatened by sickness, death, or heavy storms of thunder, my religion would not do, and I found there was something wanting, and would begin to repent my going so much to frolics, but when the distress was over, the devil and my own wicked heart, with the solicitations of my associates, and my fondness for young company, were such strong allurements, I would again give way, and thus I got to be wild and rude, at the same time kept up my rounds of secret prayer and reading...I could not satisfy myself with my diversions and in the midst of my mirth sometimes would have such a sense of my lost and undone condition that I would wish myself from the company, and after it was over when I went home, would make promises that I would attend no more on these frolics, and would beg forgiveness for hours and hours; but when I came to the temptation again, I would give way; no sooner would I hear the music and drink a glass of wine, but I would find my mind elevated and soon proceed to any sort of merriment or diversion...but when I returned from my carnal mirth I was as guilty as ever... I was one of the most unhappy creatures on earth (137-138).

Alline goes on to describe the ways in which he found himself doing things that he didn't really want to be doing. Even or especially when he was the ringleader, the wild man and life of the party, he took no satisfaction and instead was riddled with guilt and regret. To onlookers, he appeared happy and carefree. But Alline understood his own behaviors; he knew his vulnerability to music, wine, and women. He recognized and even accepted that his actions would lead to the next rounds of regret and recrimination.

James offers the example of S. H. Hadley, who described himself as "a homeless, friendless, dying, drunkard" who feels utterly broken (159). Hadley reveals that he had a list of "I'll nevers" that included never being a tramp and never being cornered. If those ever were to come to pass, Hadley promised himself he would "find a home at the bottom of the river" (159). But when he did find himself cornered and living as a tramp, he wasn't able to walk more than a quarter of the way to the river. It was after not having eaten for days and suffering from delirium tremens that he had a conversion experience.

We'll leave the Oxford graduate, Alline, and Hadley for now but return to them after exploring James's account of "world sickness" and the contemporary diagnosis of Substance Use Disorder from the *Diagnostic and Statistical Manual of Mental Disorders*.[14] The graduate's, Alline's, and Hadley's experiences will add depth and detail to the more clinical language.

The Five Stages of World Sickness

If the healthy minded tend to view the world through rose tinted glasses and actively and willfully deny the reality of evil, the sick souls or morbid minded take evil as the very essence of life. Evil has religious connotations, so it might be better to substitute badness or disappointment. Those who have morbid minds will always see the glass half empty and containing something bitter or toxic. As James says, if the healthy-minded are born with a bottle of champagne to their credit, the morbid minded are born right on their misery threshold (110). They will tend to move and live on the darker side of their misery lines. They tend to say No to what life has to offer because they become incapable of feeling and generating joy. In the worst cases, they become extremely melancholic and morbid. The sick souls are the people whom James understands best in some ways, because he and other members of his family lived on that darker side of the line. Sick souls will suffer what James calls "world sickness," which can develop and spread throughout a person's life. As a psychologist today might say, it is a progressive condition. Addiction is one particular form world sickness may take.

Sick souls become governed by fear-thought. More people, places, and things pose challenges, dangers, and threats. As a consequence, the material, social, and spiritual dimensions of sick souls suffer greatly. More pieces of their selves become inconsistent and fragmented, which produces confusion and alienation. All of this, in turn, contributes to fear-thought that continues to cycle unchecked. A sick soul is best understood as having a divided self or being a deeply divided person. A person is at war with themself, wanting contradictory things and willing to go to nearly any length to get those things. In the worst cases, it as if each part of a self wants to silence, banish, or even kill the other.

The sick souls or morbid minded cleave into two groups. The first type suffers from a maladjustment to the world. A person's inner attitudes are out of alignment with the external world. A person who previously experienced happiness or joy doing certain activities no longer feels pleasure in them. The shine is off. This is the first phase of world sickness. Call this "joy chilled." When something previously enjoyable no longer ignites a spark in a person, he may feel some confusion. A person may feel there is something wrong with them. They may wonder why they can't snap out of it or pull themself up. They might try to explain it away by saying they're just too tired, stressed, distracted, or pulled in too many directions. These may all be true and when they are less harried and stressed, the joy may return. This type of morbidity is manageable or curable; with certain attitude adjustments, one can right or balance themself.

If the stress, fatigue, and distraction continue, they may slide further down the misery scale to the second phase "joy destroyed." Here the situation is becoming more dire because a person becomes less able and willing to recognize what James calls the "natural goods" of love, friendship, connection, and purpose. The sentiments that had accompanied these dry up and turn to dust. Like the previous stage of "joy chilled," this phase is manageable. It takes greater effort though because the sentiments lack their usual motivational oomph. They might find themself doing the same things because they understand that they should. That *should* can return to a *want* to do, which stokes the motivating sentiments and produces at least some pleasure from the "natural goods."

The second type of sick soul or morbid minded suffers from the more devastating forms of world sickness. A person of this type believes the wrongness, bitterness, disappointment, or evil is part of him and the world. No amount of adjustment of attitude can manage this morbidity. One's inner state may be just a reflection or response to the fact that the world and all its people are not kind. James describes this view of the world and our place in it as pathological melancholy, which itself has three stages, each of which is more horrifying than the previous.

The first stage of pathological melancholy is anhedonia, which means no pleasure or joy. A lack of joy, or more accurately, an inability to generate joy, characterizes this stage. It isn't only pleasure that's diminished or missing. Other cares and concerns are missing. Activities, people, and places that had brought joy, or a sense of connection, meaning, and identity are met with a cold indifference. Put another way, a person starts not to care about some of the most important and central material, social, and spiritual dimensions of himself.

The second stage of pathological melancholy actively cultivates or generates angst and anguish. Call this stage "active anguish." People in this stage navigate the world with irritation, resentment, exasperation, anxiety, and fear. People present these attitudes toward the world because it is how they experience the world. James describes people in this stage as having a consciousness choked with evil. The negative emotions in this stage can be directed at different objects. James cites the Russian novelist Tolstoy as having a melancholy that is directed to objective questions such as, "Is there any value in living? What's the meaning of life? Why do we humans even exist?" These questions have a very wide scope; they're less personal but generate huge angst because they seem unanswerable. The other object to which a person can direct all his negative emotions is his own self or person. James offers John Bunyan, an English minister and author of *The Pilgrim's Progress*, as an example of this sort. He rails about all the bad and terrible things that have happened to him. He takes himself to be full of an inner pollution or to be the plague. Everything that happens is about him. He is the sort who, when tripping over a tree root, will believe the tree root tripped him. James says it is typical of this sort of person to be jealous or resentful of animals because they don't have the capacity to experience this sort of torment and suffering (126). The person in this stage tends to believe that no one else could possibly ever suffer as acutely as he does.

The final stage of pathological melancholy is the most extreme. James identifies this stage as "panic fear." This is the stage James knows best because he lived it as a young man and brushed up against it again later in his life. In this stage, a person fears everything in the universe. Fear is the only emotion a person has; it completely swamps a person's rational capacity such that he is reduced to a quivering mass of fear that is blood freezing and heart stopping. I quote at length in order to capture the desperation of this stage:

> I went one evening into a dressing room in the twilight to procure some article that was there; when suddenly there fell upon me without any warning, just as if it came out of the darkness, a horrible fear of my own existence. Simultaneously there arose in my mind the image of an epileptic patient whom I had seen in the asylum, a black haired youth with greenish skin... who used to sit all day on one of the benches... with his knees drawn up against his chin....He sat there like a sort of sculptured Egyptian cat or Peruvian mummy, moving nothing but his black eyes and looking absolutely non-human. This image and my fear entered a combination with each other. *That shape am I*, I felt, potentially....There was such a horror of him, and such a perception of my own merely momentary discrepancy from him...that I became a mass of quivering fear. After this the universe was changed for me altogether. I awoke morning after morning with a horrible dread at the pit of my stomach, and with a sense of the insecurity of life that I never knew before, and that I have never felt since (119-120).

The writer continues that the fear and anxiety were so severe that had he not clung to familiar Bible verses, he would have gone completely insane. William James later acknowledged that he himself was the author of that passage. I will return to this experience later because James's understanding of his ascent from this terrifying place is a consequence of his willingness to have faith, which was a conversion for him that I will discuss in the following chapter.

World sickness negatively affects a person's material, social, and spiritual self. Prolonged stress and fear take an enormous toll. Those who are completely governed by fear-thought are constantly in fight or flight mode, which releases excessive amounts of cortisol in the brain. More and more things and situations are taken as objects of fear. Severely pessimistic people have shorter life spans than people who are optimistic. Social relations become harder to cultivate and maintain. They, too, become sources of stress and anxiety, which prompt many to pare them. As people pare relationships, they become more remote and less practiced in the social arts. Common ordinary interactions may seem foreign. Pessimistic people who focus on grievances tend to ruminate. Often they will put everything under a microscope in order to focus on each excruciating detail. Each detail may become emblematic of all that is wrong with a person, or others, or the world writ large. As a person's world of social relations, interests, and pursuits shrink, it becomes easier to adopt of an attitude of resignation. Why bother to try anything when everything will just end in failure because that's just how it is?

Substance Use Disorder

James's five stages of world sickness—joy chilled, joy destroyed, anhedonia, active anguish, and panic fear—is one way to understand the trajectory of addiction. Combining

James's five stages of world sickness with the diagnostic criteria for a Substance Use Disorder (SUD) provides a compelling account of the suffering that is central to addiction. A SUD is a pattern of troubling or problem-causing use over a period of 12 months. The diagnosis comprises 11 criteria that fall into four categories—impaired control, social impairment, risky use, and pharmacological indicators. A person who meets 2-3 criteria has a diagnosis of a mild SUD, 3-4 a moderate SUD, and 6 or more a severe SUD.

Impaired control includes:

- Taking more of a substance or over a longer period of time than intended.
- Having a persistent desire or making unsuccessful attempts to cut down or control use.
- Spending increased time acquiring, using, or recovering from using a substance.
- Increasing desire or craving for a substance.

Social impairment includes:

- Failing to fulfill major social role obligations at work, home, school, etc.
- Continuing to use despite consistent or recurrent interpersonal or social problems.
- Reducing or giving up on important social, work, recreational activities.

Risky use includes:

- Using in situations in which it is physically hazardous.
- Continuing to use knowing that the use is causing significant physical or psychological problems.

Pharmacological indicators include:

- Experiencing changes in tolerance either needing more of the substance to achieve effects or having less effect with the usual amounts.
- Experiencing withdrawal effects particular to a substance or using some of the substance to stave off withdrawal effects.[15]

The four categories of impaired control, social impairment, risky use, and pharmacological indicators reflect the familiar claim that addiction is a biopsychosocial condition. Addiction involves one's body (not just limited to the brain), psychological states (which include what James calls "spiritual"), and social relations. Put in more Jamesian terms, addiction affects every dimension of a person. This is why James's conception of self/person is so helpful in coming to understand why individuals develop addictions and what possibilities may be more effective for recovery.

Recall that James claims that different aspects of the empirical self (material, social, and spiritual) are not separable and distinct things but rather different emphases or perspectives. The eleven criteria of SUD map onto at least one or more aspects of the empirical self. Consider taking more of a substance than intended, having a persistent desire to cut down or quit, and having an increased desire for a substance. Each of these involves the spiritual self. There are clashing desires of wanting to stop and wanting more of the substance. There's a mismatch between what a person claims to want to do and their willingness to act on those desires and intentions. The desires for particular substances and behaviors may first encroach upon, over-shadow, and finally dwarf other desires as an addiction progresses. The increased time spent acquiring, using, and recovering from use takes up more and more of a person's attention. If the spiritual self is "the house of interest," a person moving along the spectrum of a mild to moderate to severe SUD has a house in which every room is organized around that cycle.

The criteria about social impairment align not only with the social self, but also with the spiritual and material dimensions. Not meeting the social roles with which a person most closely identifies can be devastating. Giving up important social relations means losing the identities they bring. When others no longer regard a person as having good standing in a group or having the identities they once did, the loss is very real. The lack of acknowledgment, recognition, and respect can be unbearable. It may seem a form of punishment causing further damage to the relationships. It is a social death. The problems that follow from continued use such as losing family and straining friendships are simultaneously social and material. A person may become a source of shame for his family. Many of us will direct that shame right back at ourselves.

The criteria under risky use and pharmacological indicators attach most directly to the material self but also in important ways to the social self. Tolerance and withdrawal are full-bodied phenomena. It goes without saying the brain is an important organ in addiction. Different drugs target different neurotransmitters and areas of the brains, bringing about different effects. Some drugs excite and amplify, others mellow and calm, others invite hallucinations, and yet others have dissociative effects. Tolerance is how much of a substance or behavior a person needs in order to achieve desired effects. Withdrawal effects are bodies screaming for drugs. They are also minds screaming either in anticipation of physical or psychological agony. But addiction isn't all or only in the brain. Hands shake, capillaries burst, hearts race, mouths water, intestines twist, and bowels release. Withdrawal is a particular sort of physical hazard that accompanies addiction. Greater chances of being injured while walking, driving, and riding bicycles while intoxicated are physical hazards. One is more vulnerable to physical attacks and assault because intoxication impedes our ability to rationally assess risk.

Continuing to use knowing it causes significant physical and psychological harms involves the spiritual self. That knowledge can be utterly debilitating because one understands the harm he is causing himself. Many people assume that knowledge of the harms of addiction would be sufficient reasons to stop, but this is frequently not the case. Knowledge of the risks of addition is often inchoate; it isn't full blown and obvious. It might hide around the edges of the consciousness. An addict may have incentive to willfully ignore this inconvenient fact. These pieces of self-knowledge are somewhere in his stream of consciousness, and it may either exacerbate his problem or help to alleviate it. It will all depend on what he does with it.

World Sickness, SUDs, and Addicts' Suffering

The stages of World Sickness and the criteria of Substance Use Disorder can be helpfully combined to understand the Oxford graduate, Alline, and Hadley. Each of them suffers one of the more serious stages of world sickness with accompanying degrees of divisions between parts of their selves. Alline and Hadley both seem between the stages of active anguish and panic fear while the young Oxford graduate toes right up to active anguish. Each also meets a significant number of the criteria for a SUD. Hadley is suffering from delirium tremens, which is a form of alcohol withdrawal. He views himself as utterly broken, which is one way to understand not having the social and familial roles and attendant obligations. He makes no reference to attempts to quit, but as we shall see, he comes up with a plan to stop drinking for good this time, which indicates there had been unsuccessful prior attempts.

The young Oxford graduate and Alline admit to having tried numerous times to cut down or quit entirely. Their desires to stop drinking or engaging in carnal pleasures were persistent. Each is able to identify the ways they are failing to meet social or work obligations. They each recognize the tolls their alcohol use takes, but they continue to use. The Oxford graduate feels acute shame at not living up to his potential and making the best of his education. He knows that his own life isn't up to scratch. That's the inescapable fact he confronts every day.

Alline's case is especially interesting. From all outward appearances, Alline seems to have it all. Who wouldn't

want to trade places with Alline? But underneath the frivol-
ity was a deep-seated misery that was invisible to others.
Maintaining the charade of being happy and acting as if
everything is perfect while being absolutely miserable is
utterly and completely exhausting. It can also become
debilitating. Anyone who has ever been addicted to drugs
or alcohol or to gambling knows this warfare and the toll
it takes. We remain willing to pay that toll long after our
accounts have run dry.

Alline, like many who are addicted, is full of shame and
self-loathing. Making and breaking promises to himself
was typical. Each promise made holds hope that this time
it will be different. Each promise broken confirms he is
a bad and weak person. An addict barters with himself,
"Only two drinks today," or "I will not go out more than
once this week." When these negotiations break down, an
addict usually can offer a raft of rationalizations, 'Well, I
only had four drinks and usually I have six," and "This was
a special event; I meant I would only go out once a week
during a regular week." For Alline, the beautiful women
and the solicitations of his associates would lure him back
to a wild lifestyle. Alline was especially adept at rationaliza-
tion. Surely, he told himself, if he could avoid drinking and
swearing, God would be forgiving or even accepting. Not
even God would want to deny all pleasures, right?

Addicts also get very good at minimizing the consequences of our actions; we can rewrite any event so it
does not seem so bad. At times we can truly excel and
make those awful consequences seem like fun. All of this

becomes exhausting and many of us get tangled up in guilt. Unfortunately, this guilt does not often translate into taking responsibility. Thus, we are often miserable, so that each of us says of himself as Alline did, "I was one of the most unhappy creatures on earth."

Inconsistency or lack of congruence in what we want and how we live is a hallmark of addiction. Payment for that inconsistency is always due. No matter how we act, we will somehow be going against what we profess to want. When we drink, a voice in our heads is saying, "You really do not want to be doing this." When we don't drink, the voice says, "You know you want to drink and you can." No matter what we do, we will see ourselves as failures or victims or wronged or long suffering. We will probably see ourselves as all of these simultaneously, and that serves as justification for us to use our drugs or engage in our addictive behaviors. Each of us is caught in what James calls the "stages of world sickness."

In each phase of world sickness, a person becomes more shrunken. It is as if people collapse into themselves. If expansiveness characterizes healthy-mindedness, contraction is the hallmark of world sickness. Various dimensions of a person's empirical self are lost, cast off, or left behind. Some pieces may be intentionally cast off because they bring too much pain and agony. A person remembering how he used to be or what he used to be able to do is a special torment. Considering his past dreams, goals, and aspirations and now recognizing they are well beyond reach knocks him down. Losing or discarding our passions and dreams that gave life purpose is utterly alienating. Spiritual selves shrivel; fear and panic dwarf intellectual and moral concerns. When he catches glimpses of his past self, especially when he was engaged, connected, and active in the world, he sees a person who knew who he was and what mattered to him. Comparing himself now to that person, he may feel as if he has utterly failed.

Some of these wounds may be self-inflicted, and hence a source of special torment. He may not recognize this and instead will blame others, which stokes resentment. There may be times when he feels some of his responsibility, and he may either avert his gaze or blame himself. That blame may not translate into acting differently and assuming appropriate responsibility. It may accelerate his self-loathing and shame. Each of these self-inflicted wounds may be relatively minor at first. Taken together over a period of time, their cumulative effect can be devastating. As the misery progresses, one loses perspective and becomes less able to judge what is a tolerable loss or wound and what is not. Each one of these wounds is a complicated web of material, social, and spiritual dimensions of self. Putting it slightly differently, all losses start to be put on par with each other. Whether it is losing a job, feeling snubbed by a friend, or not being able to fix the kitchen faucet, each is deeply grievous.

At the final stage of panic fear, where fear-thought has completely flooded a person's self, it becomes impossible to draw a line between what is subjective/in him and what is objective/outside of him. Everything has collapsed into a sea of anguish and despair; that is the horrible nature of reality. He is misery and the world is misery. It's all misery. At this point, he may vacillate between the two extremes of "it's all my fault," and "none of it is my fault." This wild swinging seems never to stop. Living hyperbolic contradictory beliefs is exhausting and debilitating, creating more misery. It will be very hard for a person to slow that pendulum and come to rest in the middle where he may be able to apprehend what's appropriately in his control and responsibility and what is not. The wild swinging most surely drains a person's willingness to even try to do something differently.

Addicts can experience any or all of these types of world sicknesses and their accompanying losses. There are many forms of suffering, and no one form and no one stage of world sickness is emblematic for all. James's notion of the misery threshold is useful here. Some people have a much lower tolerance for suffering, and will be motivated sooner rather than later to make changes to reduce their suffering. Other people tolerate more for longer, and their world sickness may progress at a slow and steady rate or may have bursts of acceleration. The use of some drugs, for example, may lead more quickly to a sort of abject terror and paranoia. When you are drained of hope, color, and life, James would say, you have the chance to fundamentally transform your habitual center of personal energy. You are primed for a conversion.

Is this to say that everyone must reach such depths of despair as James himself did and that Bill Wilson wrote was almost always required? No, it isn't. Recall Ryan from the previous chapter. While healthy-minded and optimistic in many ways, changes in the conditions of their life and changes within themself made them more vulnerable to fear. They perhaps experienced joy chilled or even joy destroyed. Keep in mind what James says about people having very different misery thresholds. In response to some loss of hope, some people will be willing to be transformed. These might be the people who meet only 2 or 3 of the SUD criteria and hence have a mild disorder. These people may be able to walk their use back by making different kinds of adjustments in their lives. Some of us stop our drug use well before we lose jobs, partners, families, and dreams. We will seek ways to keep the various dimensions of our selves in a sustainable balance. All parts of us may not be in perfect harmony nor are they in outright war with each other. Balances are dynamic, though, which means they are constantly changing in response to a changing world and to changes within us. What is a sustainable and healthy balance in the short term may become less healthy or maladaptive in the longer term.

Other people can suffer a significant loss of hope and color but still stay somewhere in the comfort zone of their misery threshold. These may be people with a moderate SUD. Others can sustain these loses and continue to use even as their divided selves are engaged in active warfare. Others will need to feel total and complete misery and may have landed at the severe end of the SUD spectrum. They may be like Alline and feel they are the most miserable creatures on earth. They may be Hadley, completely destitute and alone. They can fail to live up to their own expectations, and feel as if they are wasting their lives, like the young Oxford graduate. Each person has her own misery threshold, and when it is crossed, that is the rock bottom *for her*. It is crucial that really terrible and debilitating consequences not be taken as models for what it means to hit rock bottom. If someone were to claim, "well, I never lost my family, job, or all my money and in fact had a lot of money so I don't have to be done drinking yet and I am not an alcoholic," this would be distorted thinking that could lead to truly life-shattering consequences for that person. This is a dangerous belief that may keep them from seeking help and making changes sooner rather than later. Rock bottoms vary greatly, and no one is more legitimate than any other. Rock bottoms are deeply personal; each individual must come to recognize what it is for her. That may be the point where she is willing to live on a *maybe* she can do things differently. If she believes in that possibility, she may become *willing* to start doing things differently.

Having said this about differences in rock bottoms, the depth of a person's rock bottom may have a direct effect on the type of conversion they will experience. Higher rock bottoms—those who have a low tolerance for misery—might be more susceptible to what James calls a voluntary or volitional conversion. Deeper rock bottoms that leave sufferers with nothing left might be more susceptible to the sudden sort of conversion that Bill W. experienced. The process of conversions and the speed at which they occur are the subjects of the next chapter.

Chapter Five

Conversions and the Hot Spot of Consciousness

*To be converted, to be regenerated, to receive grace, to
experience religion, to gain assurance, are some many phrases
which denote the process, gradual or sudden, by which a
self hitherto divided, and consciously wrong inferior and
unhappy, becomes unified and consciously right and superior
and happy, in consequence of its firmer hold upon religious
realities. This at least is what conversion signifies in general
terms, whether or not we believe that a direct divine operation
is needed to bring such a moral change about.*

WILLIAM JAMES

How do conversions happen? Does a force outside a person
cause the change or does the change come from within? So
much rides on this question for those who struggle with
their use of alcohol, other drugs, and addictive behaviors.
I will first offer the cases of the conversions of the young
Oxford graduate, S.H. Hadley, and the evangelist Alline.
These are cases of people who believe God was the cause
or the author of their conversions. Their conversions were

sudden and unexpected; each felt as if something was being done to him. However, these cases represent only one type of conversion and are not emblematic of all conversions. As we shall see, there are many instances where an individual is the cause or author of his own conversion. The volitional or willful conversions often proceed with a more gradual pace. These examples show that conversions are not one-size-fits-all, but are defined by a great variety of dynamics, trajectories, and speeds. Conversions may happen suddenly or gradually. Whether a person experiences the change coming from an external source or from an internal one, what matters the most are the results of a conversion.

A Glorious Brightness

The Oxford graduate's conversion happened on a hot July day when he had been abstaining from alcohol for nearly a month. He didn't feel troubled or at odds with himself. He certainly was not thinking about God. A young lady friend sent him a book about spiritual matters in the natural world. He read the book partly with the intent of impressing her with his profound thoughts about it. He came upon a biblical verse he had read countless times but this time it made a distinct and powerful impression upon him. He described himself as feeling that God was with him at that very moment and experiencing a marvelous stillness. At the same time, he felt an acute regret at all that he had wasted or lost in his lifetime. He felt doomed until the thought gently came to him that Jesus Christ would save him. So joyous was he that the entire town heard of his conversion within 24 hours.

The day after his conversion he was working in the field during harvest. He thought to himself that he hadn't promised God he would stop drinking or even drink more moderately. He drank in his usual way to the point of intoxication. When he returned home, his sister was devastated. His pangs of remorse were acute. He knew God's work wasn't wasted but that he needed to pray. In his prayer, he notes, "I committed myself to him in the profoundest belief that my individuality was going to be destroyed, that he would take all from me, and I was willing. In such a surrender lies the secret of a holy life" (175). At that moment, alcohol no longer presented any temptation to him. The desire for his pipe lifted. He regarded his deliverance from these temptations as complete and permanent.

S. H. Hadley describes the night that he is sitting in a Harlem saloon, completely friendless and without hope. He writes,

> As I sat there thinking, I seemed to feel some great and mighty presence. I did not know then what it was. I did learn afterwards that it was Jesus, the sinner's friend. I walked up to the bar and pounded it with my fist till I made the glass rattle. Those who stood by drinking looked on with scornful curiosity. I said I would never take another drink, if I died on the street, and really I felt as though that would happen before morning. Something said, "if you want to keep that promise, go and have yourself locked up."

> I went to the nearest station house and had myself locked up.

> I was placed in a narrow cell, and it seemed as though all the demons that could find room came in that place with me. This was not all the company I had, either. No, praise the lord, that dear Spirit that came to me in the saloon was present and said, Pray (159).

Once he is released from his cell, he returns to his brother's home and then visits a mission where "the apostle to the drunkard and outcast—that man of God—Jerry M'Auley" was praying. Hadley listened to the testimony of 25 other drunkards who had given up the rum. As he was listening, he recalls,

> Oh, what a conflict was going on for my poor soul. A blessed whisper said, "Come"; the devil said, "Be careful." I halted but a moment, and then, with a breaking heart, I said, "Dear Jesus, can you help me?" Never with a mortal tongue can I describe that moment. Up until that time my soul had been filled with indescribable gloom, I felt the glorious brightness of the noonday shine into my heart (160).

Hadley goes on to describe himself as a free man from that moment onward. He never wanted another drink of whiskey.

Alline had descended into the state of panic fear. Walking in the fields, he lamented all his woes. As he reached his front door, a small but powerful voice in his mind pointed out that all his lamenting, praying, working, and reading hadn't moved him one step closer to salvation. He was as unfit to appear before God now as he had been when he first began. Absolutely devastated by this thought and spinning even more dire ones, he grabbed his Bible and opened it at random to the 38th Psalm. Like the Oxford graduate, the words took hold of him in an entirely new way. He called out for God to save him. When he did that,

> I gave all up to him to do with me as he pleased, and was willing that God should rule over me at his pleasure, redeeming love broke into my soul with repeated scriptures, with such power my whole soul seemed to be melted down with love; the burden of guilt and condemnation was gone, darkness was expelled, my heart humbled and filled with gratitude. (172).

All of this exhausted Alline, who wanted nothing more than to sleep. But the devil appeared to him and he worried that if he slept, he'd awaken in the morning to find his experience had all been a delusion. But he fell asleep. Upon waking, his first question was "Where is my God?" In that instant, Alline said his soul was awake in and with God surrounded by the arms of everlasting love (172). On that day, Alline became a Christian minister.

Conversions without a God

The stories of the Oxford graduate, Hadley, and Alline are exemplars of the "self-surrender" conversion. Each held some belief about God prior to their spiritual experience and so were inclined to believe that God directly intervened and authored their sudden changes. This possibility—of an active and providential God—was part of their worldviews or over-beliefs. The hypothesis that God intervenes in human lives worked for these three men. However, that hypothesis does not work for many people.

Can people experience a sudden change without direct intervention from God? Yes, actually, and it's important here to consider some examples of "self-surrender" conversions with no reference to a direct intervention by God. One example James offers is a man who has a sudden conversion out of a deep melancholy. The converted man is an atheist. What motivates this man, James opines, is an ethical claim about recognizing the worth and dignity of another, perhaps one whose humanity has been discounted or reviled. This is a powerful example. When we recognize that we are no different from others whom we have been encouraged to see as lesser or deviant, we change. Something similar can happen when a person who long ago squandered their sense of worth and dignity through addictive behaviors catches even a glimpse of that worth and dignity. Worth and dignity are vital moral goods many of us lose or trade away with our use. Catching a glimpse of them may ignite a desire to want to have them again. These moral goods may work as a powerful higher power.

There are numerous examples of the second type of conversions, which are called volitional or gradual conversions. These examples are important for two reasons. First, they highlight the underlying psychological process that defines all conversions. Second, they demonstrate conversions to un- or disbelief in God or any deity. This shows that religious conversions are but one type or subset of all conversions.

James discusses a nameless woman who always had a hearty dose of skepticism about a providential and all-loving God. As a young woman, she joined a church and was asked if she loved God. She reflexively answered, "Yes," but at the same time a voice inside her said she really didn't. For years she lived with guilt and shame over her lack of certainty about God. One day as she was recovering from an illness, she heard a story of a man who brutally beat his wife. She noted, "I felt the horror of the thing keenly. Instantly this thought flashed through my mind: 'I have no use for a God who permits such things'" (140). She described herself as maintaining an indifference to God with little desire to placate him.

Two more examples of gradual conversions will illuminate some of their characteristic features. The first is a conversion to greed and avarice. A young man who had inherited a sizable fortune had the great misfortune of having friends who were more than happy to drink, dine, and carouse on his purse. In short order, he lost all his money, land, and friends. Penniless and friendless, he found himself walking past the lands he used to own. Seeing what he had lost, he immediately formed the resolution he would get it all back and acquire even more holdings. No job was below him; he would do any job for money. He only spent money to invest in opportunities to make more money. He made a wise investment in cattle that enabled him to buy massive acreage. He was a miser of the highest order. Upon his death, he had amassed a sizable fortune.

It isn't just sick souls who may undergo a conversion. A healthy-minded person is more likely to experience a gradual conversion. We've already encountered one such case with the healthy-minded man who followed the Japanese Buddhist recommendation to remove worry and anger from his life. His conversion is from healthy-mindedness to an even greater healthy-mindedness. Intentionally removing worry and anger from his life, put this man in contact with something More, or Heaven as he called it. Cultivating this connection and orienting his life around it resulted in him reaping what James calls the practical fruit of the spiritual tree.

The final example of a gradual conversion is a young man who falls out of love. He describes his beloved as having a "spirit of coquetry like a cat" (142). Gaining her affection was all he ever thought about. He wanted to marry her even though he knew she wasn't right for him. For a year, he pursued her knowing she would reject him if he asked. But one morning on the way to breakfast, thinking of her and feeling his usual misery, he found himself just turning around. Back in his room, he destroyed every memento, letter, and gift. He said, "I now loathed and despised her altogether, and for myself I felt as if a load of disease had suddenly been removed from me" (142).

That James would include an example of a person falling out of love isn't surprising since he himself experienced a conversion falling in love and marrying. James met and fell in love with Alice Gibbens in 1876. At the same time he professed his love to her in person and through letters, he plunged back into the despair he had experienced in 1870. He agonized over whether he was worthy of her love. The letters between them reveal James's internal battles and his zig-zagging behavior toward her. In one letter he would advise her to leave him and travel to England; in the next he would plead with her to stay. Alice remained steadfast throughout, but she did go to Canada for a period of time. Perhaps realizing how this might devastate him, she left a compass to orient him toward her. When James asked her a second time to marry him, she accepted. They wed in a small ceremony in Boston in July 1878. Ten years later, William told Alice, "I am strong and sound and that poor diseased boy whom you raised up no longer exists. Your faith, your trust, is fully verified, and I am born again through and through....You have been right from first to last."[16] James became renewed and regenerated, a person who loved and was loved in a lifelong marriage.

I will return to these cases below. But for now, each of them involves a final moment/last straw to act as a catalyst of change. A gradual conversion may proceed in smaller fits and starts while the self-surrender sort feels like one big seismic shift. However, the result is the same. A person fundamentally changes how they are in the world.

Stream of Consciousness

We now have a catalogue of conversions. Some are sudden while others gradual. Some seem caused by a Godlike external force while others seem internally generated. Finding a God, losing a God, falling in love, falling out of love, seeking wealth, discovering the dignity and worth of others or oneself—each of these is a conversion. No matter the origin and no matter the speed, a conversion is a psychological process within a person that brings about profound change. But why and how do conversions happen?

Anyone who has ever thought their mind is a bad neighborhood that they themselves don't want to visit is already walking a path with William James. In general, we don't tend to fear brightly lit areas we can accurately survey. When everything is open to view, there's far less worry that something awful is lurking around the corner or beneath the surface. Those of us who were blackout drinkers, for example, are quite certain there are horrors just waiting to mug us, especially because we cannot remember what we had been doing. Blackouts are scary for all the obvious reasons (making horrible decisions, putting ourselves at risk, endangering others, etc.) but also because we have no memories. Our fear of not having memories may be surpassed by our fear of those memories coming back. We may perceive rough and shadowy outlines of what we did, which may just knock the wind out of us. We may want to avert our inner gaze and banish all the thoughts, feelings, and sensations that either come from what we did or what we imagine ourselves to have done. James's conception of consciousness as a stream helps to explain our bad neighborhood minds and how conversions happen.

One of the most enduring concepts James bequeathed is "stream of consciousness." This concept is necessary for understanding why, how, when, and at what speed a person may experience a conversion. The stream of consciousness is connected to James' conception of self discussed earlier. Persons are simultaneously an I and a me. The "me" part or what James calls the empirical self has material, social, and spiritual dimensions. A self is composed of these aspects interacting at all times. If a self doesn't have just one dimension, why should consciousness have just one dimension or level? James forcefully rejects the position that a person can ever command a complete and infallible view of his own mind. The mind is never completely transparent; it is never a brightly lit room where everything is on display. Rather, the mind or consciousness is a stream comprising several different but interacting elements.

In *Principles of Psychology*, James argues that different activities occur all the time in our consciousness. There are different paces to these activities; some happen slowly while others move with a greater speed. James writes of consciousness, "Like a bird's life, it seems to be made of an alternation of flights and perchings" (*PP* 237). The perchings or resting places are what he calls the substantive parts; they are the objects that are before our minds. We can hold ideas in our mind and do all sorts of things such as augment, diminish, contrast, reinvent, and interrogate them. We pay attention to these substantive parts; we are often quite intentional in what we call up to our mind's eye. The flights are the transitive parts, which are the relations and dynamics between the substantive parts. Each of these—the substantive and the transitive—are equal parts of the stream. They differ in how we treat them. When we pay attention to relations between substantive parts, those relations become substantive objects. What's crucial that the stream of consciousness is dynamic—it never stops.

In addition to the different paces of the stream, there are different areas. There are fringe parts that are just as interesting and important as what seemingly moves in the middle of the stream. These fringe areas are familiar to all of us, James claims. Trying to remember a forgotten name involves a gap that is very active. James notes, "A sort of wraith of the name is in it, beckoning us in a given direction, making us at moments tingle with the sense of closeness" (*PP* 244). When the wrong name is proposed, we reject it because it doesn't fit the mold we have of that name. At times it seems as if we are feeling our way towards that missing name, trying to remember details, make associations, etc. And then suddenly it seems to come to us. Another example is an instance of recognizing an experience as familiar but not being able to identify when it was enjoyed before. It may be a sound, taste, or a melody that feels so familiar yet eludes identification (*PP* 244).

The stream has flotsam, which is wreckage or cargo that floats along the surface, sinks deeper, or washes up to the shore. These may be memories, sensations, and interpretations of our experiences. While memories often cluster together, some of them break away only to reappear unbidden. They may seem to come out of nowhere, but they have in fact come from ourselves. There's also jetsam or the debris that is deliberately thrown overboard to lighten a load especially when in distress. All of us repress thoughts, feelings, or memories in the hopes of lightening our psychological loads. We omit, repress, rewrite, reinterpret, and revise certain experiences so that they exert a lesser toll on us. We often do this in the hopes of maintaining our image of ourselves. We go to such great lengths to *not* find ourselves out and to avoid facing what we are up against in ourselves.

Much later in his career, James returned to the topic of consciousness in *Talks to Teachers* (hereafter *TT*). He reminds his audience that whether awake or asleep, "there is some kind of consciousness going on. There is a stream, a succession of states, or waves or fields (or whatever you want to call them), of knowledge, of feeling, of desire, of deliberation, etc., that constantly pass and repass, and that constitute our inner life" (*TT* 19). James admits that explaining these states is beyond the grasp of the science of his day (and perhaps our own). But all is not lost because what we cannot explain, we may still describe. In many ways, this is what he does in *Varieties*. He describes transformations that happen within the consciousness of individuals. In *Talks to Teachers*, James claims that sensations occupy the center of the stream while thoughts and feelings occupy the margin. Any of these can shift at any time. An audience member may be concentrating intensely on what the speaker is saying, but a foot cramp will banish all thoughts and take center stage. Focal objects and activities and marginal ones may quickly or slowly trade places. The border between them may be blurry, but that is to be expected according to James. Consciousness is incessantly changing (*TT* 22).

A conversion happens when ideas, thoughts, or images in the subconscious are able to move their way into conscious awareness. It is much like something lodged in the sediment of a stream coming to the surface. The conscious and rational mind typically dominates the subconscious being ever vigilant to guard the perimeter between the two. There's a fuzzy area or what James calls a "transmarginal region," between the two. The expression, "to put something out of your mind," reveals how we try to remove unwanted, unpleasant, or even scary thoughts, feelings, or images from our awareness. When we repress thoughts in this manner, we think we have rid ourselves of them. However, they don't necessarily disappear. Rather, they go to a different place in our minds; they may be in that "transmarginal region." Under certain conditions, those thoughts, feelings, sensations, or images make themselves known. For James, the movement of ideas, images, feelings, or sensations out of the subconscious and transmarginal region into consciousness is the hallmark of a conversion.

Sudden self-surrender conversions and gradual volitional conversions share the same psychological process but progress at different speeds. In some cases, thoughts, images, and sensations explode into consciousness with such great force it seems as if they have an external cause. James calls these tsunamis or upheavals "self-surrender" conversions. Given the tremendous force of these upheavals, it is tempting to assume some outside power is at work. Alline, Hadley, and the young Oxford graduate describe their experiences as if something is being done to them by an external source. Given that the experiences come unbidden, they are interpreted as surrender to something beyond themselves. Bill Wilson's conversion follows this same trajectory.

In other cases, the ideas, images, and feelings slowly work their way through that transmarginal region and into consciousness. These conversions are what James calls volitional or gradual. Volitional conversions unfold gradually over a period of time, and the person's intentions play an active role in the process. Even in the volitional conversions, there will often be "ah ha" moments or mini self-surrenders. In each type of conversion, people become whole and unified, which is itself a "practical fruit of the spiritual tree." This unification enables people to reap other such fruits.

Some people have wider fields of interest and attention than others. The longer and wider the fields, the greater the region of the margins. Large transmarginal regions will provide more opportunities for incursions of thoughts and feelings into conscious awareness. Thus, the difference between gradual and sudden conversions is not that the latter involve divine intervention, but rather is due to the psychological peculiarity that some people have larger transmarginal regions where work goes on subconsciously.

Sensing an Incompleteness and
Coming to Have a Positive Vision

James claims there are two other things are required for a person to have a conversion. The first is a recognition of the present incompleteness or wrongness from which the person is eager to escape (164). Clearly, the Oxford graduate, Hadley, and Alline could list all the ways that their lives had gone off the rails. Each of Alline's numerous unsuccessful attempts to quit revealed how incomplete and unfulfilling his life was. The Oxford graduate recognized that his life was a disappointment to himself and to others. Hadley's rocketing down his list of "I'll nevers" reinforced his view that his life was not worth living. People struggling with addiction often have a very clear sense of how their lives are incomplete or broken. They see their own disappointments and failures. They perceive their broken promises to themselves and the havoc those have wrought. They see exactly how dismal their life is. Many of us are over-achievers in taking stock of the manifold wrongness in our lives. All of these thoughts, we might say, are in the stream of consciousness. They are so plentiful and enormous that they form a tremendous jam.

Such a tremendous jam can be sanity and life threatening, as those who suffer from pathological melancholy or world sickness know too well. When disappointments, negative experiences, grievances, and aggravations fill one's mind to the point of excluding alternatives, there will always be great suffering. A person may genuinely not care what happens to them. That suffering may well prompt a person to wonder whether life is worth living, as I will discuss in the next chapter.

While there may be some denial about how wrong or how incomplete our lives are, those ideas or sensations often take root in one's subconscious mind or "transmarginal region" where they slowly blossom. It is utterly exhausting to inhabit that wrongness and incompleteness. The guard-dog quality of the rational and conscious mind may break down, which primes the pump for a conversion. However, something else needs to be present so that a person does not get stuck viewing an infinite tape of all that is wrong with his life. Such a loop is debilitating for most people.

The second idea or notion a person must have is a positive ideal or vision that he "longs to compass" or orient his life toward (165). A positive vision of life must replace the negative one with its sense of wrongness and incompleteness. Coming to have a positive vision is a challenge for most who have been mired in negative and even debilitating views about themselves and the world. A person who hopes to escape or transform the incompleteness of her present life still has some care for herself. She has not reached the point of becoming indifferent to her own welfare. Someone who develops an addiction later in life might be able to draw from her experiences before her addiction became so severe to generate a positive ideal. Imagination enables us to draw from the past and chart a course for a future. However, not everyone will have positive past experiences that can function in this way.

One of the reasons why mutual support groups such as AA can be so helpful to people trying to stop using is that they can see others who have changed their use. They can hear about the ways others understood their own incompleteness and wrongness. Perhaps even more importantly, hearing stories about others' transformations helps to fire the imagination and renew one's hope. Someone else's transformation may function as a positive ideal. At some point, a person needs to imagine possibilities for herself, begin to hope for those things, and take concrete action to make them actual. Doing this marks an important change from saying No to drugs and alcohol to embracing life with a resounding Yes.

People who have dwelled for so long in their own wrongness and incompleteness may be unable to recognize anything positive. Or they may even be terrified by the thought of imagining or hoping for something positive. Those who have progressed to the panic fear stage of world sickness may have reached a point of indifference to themselves. A person is indifferent to her own self when she has a complete lack of interest and care about herself. A person becomes fatalistic—everything that has happened to her was bound to happen so the outcome is inevitable. Fatalism driven by indifference is perhaps the lowest point a person can reach. Why bother to care when nothing she does matters or changes anything? Will this person even care about finding a positive ideal?

James recognized that some people have sunk so low and fallen out of regular human traffic that they need help to be rescued. James, drawing from the founder of The Salvation Army, notes the first thing that must happen is "making them feel as if some decent human being cares enough for them to take an interest in the question whether they are to rise or sink" (footnote p. 160). A person who is indifferent to herself no longer cares whether she rises or sinks. She can't generate enough care for and interest in her own welfare and instead needs to draw some energy from someone else. This is the moral equivalent of a jump start. Each of us may provide that jump start for another and not even know it. Another can provide that jump start, but each person needs to keep the engine running.

The Habitual Center of Personal Energy and the Hot Spot of Consciousness

What changes do conversions cause? A conversion changes a person's habitual center of personal energy or "the hot spot of consciousness." A person who experiences a conversion alters the set of commitments, beliefs, values, and behaviors around which he organizes his life. Converted people also amend how they see themselves, orienting their lives away from the incompleteness and wrongness to something positive that they begin to claim for their own. This is why James calls converted people regenerated, rejuvenated, and reborn.

Here the question of divine intervention rises. Who authors these experiences or causes these changes in people? As a man of science—physician and psychologist—and as a philosopher, James explains conversions consistently with science, without making any assumptions about outside forces such as God or gods causing conversions. For this reason, James offers several examples of conversions away from religious belief to unbelief. Those examples are important because they reveal the dynamics of conversions and the changes they bring about in a person's actions and self-understanding. Since the subject of *Varieties* is religious experience, it makes sense that the majority of conversion examples are people in whom spiritual impulses or beliefs become central. It would be a mistake, however, to see James as endorsing the view that a God, higher power, or something More is necessary for a person to be converted. Assumptions about divine forces and God or gods are the subject of over-beliefs, which James scrupulously avoided. While some people may feel as if there is some outside force changing them or guiding them, James argues there is no proof that this force/God causes the conversion and subsequent changes in a person. The most we are licensed to conclude is that conversions are psychological processes but not divine ones.

Psychology and theology agree that the force driving the change is seemingly outside the conscious individual. A psychological account recognizes that the subconscious is outside the scope of rational consciousness but is still a part of consciousness as a whole. The subconscious cannot be assayed by the rational consciousness in any determinate way. A theological explanation locates the force in a supernatural power or deity outside of the person. As a scientist, James withholds his assent to this hypothesis because it cannot be proven. Science can document conversions, but cannot prove that a god causes them. James, however, does leave open the possibility of a God or gods by noting that a subliminal or subconscious self does not necessarily preclude the presence of a deity. He grants that it is logically conceivable that,

> *if there be* higher spiritual agencies that can directly touch us, the psychological condition of their doing so might be our possession of a subconscious region which alone would yield access to them. The hubbub of waking life might close a door which in the dreamy subliminal might remain ajar and open (emphases original 189-190).

It is important to note James's use of a conditional; he says, "*if* there be higher spiritual agencies." He does not make a definitive claim there are such powers.

The God hypothesis works for those who already believe or come from a background in which those beliefs have currency. Spiritual experiences belong to individuals who get to be experts on their own experiences. But those without belief in a personified, agential god may still have life altering conversions in which the driving force is some thought, belief, feeling, image, or intuition coming from within themselves.

I conclude this chapter with another conversion that William James experienced as a young man prior to meeting Alice Gibbens. This conversion had both sudden and volitional elements. Recall that James used his own experience as a young physician encountering and recognizing

HIGHER AND FRIENDLY POWERS

himself in an asylum patient as an example of the worst
sort of pathological melancholy. In 1870, William James
suffered severe panic-fear. In its stranglehold, James was
at risk of losing himself and any connection to the external
world. For at least two years prior to that moment, James
had been caught in a deepening spiral of crashing, making
resolutions, recovering some ground, and then crashing
even more deeply. His physical health was precarious, and
he was regularly wracked with pain. He lost a cousin whom
he loved dearly, and he was not on any career path. He
spent much of his time reading his father's religious texts
as well as Buddhist and philosophical texts. His physical,
social, and material selves were frayed and frantic. On the
night he had his own acute spiritual crisis (as his father had
had decades earlier and about which he had been reading),
he was overcome by a fear that was "so invasive and powerful that if I had not clung to scripture texts....I think I would
have gone insane" (128). James clung to something familiar
as everything else in the world felt alien. James understood
his extreme melancholia as a religious phenomenon in the
sense of an individual spiritual crisis. This experience and
his understanding of it underpins *Varieties*.

Reflecting on this experience later in his life, James understood himself to have made a choice to believe in free
will. Everything is not predetermined and fated to happen.
James said of himself, "my first act of free will shall be to
believe in free will."[17] James made a deal with himself, which
in hindsight saved both his sanity and life. He wrote that
he would stop focusing solely on abstract speculation and

contemplation. Instead, he would "voluntarily cultivate the feeling of moral freedom, by reading books favorable to it, as well as by acting."[18]

Action is the crucial component of this self-made bargain. Voluntarily cultivating a feeling or interest is an action; it is about shifting or adding to the spiritual self. Cultivating a willingness to believe and taking action on these beliefs are themes in James's life and work. It is how he emerged from his downward spiral in 1870, and fended it off again when he met Alice, and periodically throughout his life. James came to realize that acting as if his actions make a difference does in fact make a difference.

Those of us who struggle with addiction may wonder whether we have free will. The language of much addiction research makes it seem that we do not. Addiction has been called a disease of free will. Other researchers describe the brain as being hijacked or commandeered by alcohol, drugs, and other addictive behaviors. We may come to believe that relapse is inevitable because that is what always happens; this is the characteristic dynamic of addiction. What would it be like to believe in free will—that our actions can and will make a difference? What if we made the bargain that James did, choosing to believe that our actions make a real difference and discovering that that belief itself makes a real difference? This is one way to understand faith, which is the subject of the next chapter.

Chapter Six

Willingness to Live
on a Maybe

*At the bottom of the whole concern of both morality and
religion is the matter of our acceptance of the universe.
Do we accept it only in part and grudgingly, or
heartily and altogether?*

WILLIAM JAMES

James claims that in both gradual and sudden conversions,
self-surrender and letting go are necessary. The self-surrender in the gradual conversions seems a gentle and soft
putting down. It is done over a course of time in smaller
degrees. It may be hard to recognize at first. Its effects,
however, are very noticeable over time. Sometimes that
letting go is a matter of utter defeat, a crying "uncle" as it
were. Other times it is an act of defiance as we saw with S.H.
Hadley and Bill Wilson. These are all ways of surrendering
and letting go. Many people find the notions of surrendering and letting go in AA objectionable. The first step of AA,
which is admitting we were powerless over alcohol and that
our lives had become unmanageable, is descriptively accu-

rate for many of us. We did often drink or use more than we intended. Once we started, we may not have been able to stop. We often could recognize how drinking or using disrupted our lives to the point where we were no longer able to recognize ourselves and the course of our lives. The objection to the language of powerlessness seems to come from its extension to all other areas of our lives and to the purported "cure" of our ailment. We are powerless to cure ourselves. The "cure" for our powerlessness comes from putting everything in a God's hands. That God, once we relinquish all power, can restore us to sanity if we turn our lives over to him and let him care for us. Later in Step 11, we pray for knowledge of God's will for us. We become empowered when we can follow the divine will. On this view, it seems as if any power we possess on our own is only the sort that will get us into great difficulties; only power directed by and towards God will save us from our suffering. In AA, one needs to surrender in defeat to have any possibility for recovery. This view of God, his powers, and human relations to him is entirely a product of a specific set of over-beliefs, namely, those of Bill Wilson and other early members of AA.

What if, instead, self-surrender and letting go enable new activities and ways of being in the world that are empowering and transformative? The idea of faith presents an obstacle for many trying to change their addictive behavior. One of the greatest legacies of James—and perhaps the most liberating—is his more expansive conception of faith. Faith is not belief in a set of doctrines. It does not require any certainty. For James, faith is a willingness to live on possibilities. To have faith is to act when the results are uncertain. Acting in the face of uncertainty may help to bring about certainty. Moreover, faith runs through all areas of our lives. Faith can be about anything from mundane matters to the deeply existential concerns of people struggling daily with addiction. James understood the magnitude of faith in the choice to continue living.

Surrendering and Renouncing

The term "surrender" seems to imply giving something up involuntarily, which results in some sort of constraint. People charged with crimes must surrender to the police. They may then have to surrender their passports as a condition of bail. Surrender suggests punishment and confinement rather than liberation. I prefer the term "renounce." Renouncing beliefs and actions is stronger and more morally significant than merely changing them. There is a level of conscious attention and engagement in renouncing in which a person disavows or no longer pledges allegiance to behaviors or views about the world and her place in it. To renounce is to adopt a new moral stance towards one's self.

When a person renounces something, she is saying something no longer belongs to or is a part of her. She puts down particular beliefs, values, attitudes, or actions. She is no longer being and participating in the world in the same ways. If I renounce some of my past actions, I am saying that I do not approve of them for myself and perhaps not for others. I disapprove of and want no longer to do those sorts of things. Some of us renounce parts of ourselves, often phrasing it along the lines of "I don't want to be that type of person anymore." More specifically, some might say, "I don't want to be the drunk parent who misses my kids growing up. I don't want to be the reason why my kids won't have friends over to the house." Renunciation involves a person's various social, material, and spiritual selves realigning themselves, often giving selves that have been silenced, squashed, or sequestered opportunities to express themselves. When we pay attention to these and allow different interests and aspirations to exert themselves, all aspects of our person may change. James claimed that when the spiritual self—the seat of interest and attention—changes, the individual changes. The intentionality behind renouncing transforms a person such that he may start to see possibilities where before he had only seen preordained awful outcomes.

Renunciation is actual only when a person begins to consistently act in different ways. For example, James renounced his tendency to live, read, and work on abstractions and contemplative matters shortly after his experience in the asylum in 1870. He chose to act differently and to believe his actions made a difference. Another example is the man who followed a Japanese Buddhist recommendation to let go of anger and worry and renounce them. He no longer clutched them as he had in the past. In putting these beliefs down and changing his actions, he made room for other beliefs and actions in his life. This is how he came to recognize a Heaven within himself. It was only by throwing down his worry and fear that he could grasp this Heaven.

Many people struggling with addiction often tightly clutch core beliefs about their drug or alcohol use, their prospects for a future, and the worth of their own lives. They are committed to views of themselves as unsalvageable because of their long lists of failures and transgressions. These beliefs form the dominant part of a person's habitual center of personal energy. Clutch anything tightly for a long time, and one experiences an incredible cramp. Addicts experience an existential cramp. Or to put it in more Jamesian terms, all the material, social, and spiritual dimensions of a person are cramping. This cramping is extraordinarily painful. Being able to loosen one's grip even just a bit may alleviate some of the pain; it may be a first step. It most likely will not be a painless first step even though it is putting a burden down.

Renouncing, especially in the sudden tsunami type of conversion, excludes hedging one's bets. One cannot both become a new person and hold onto old ways of doing and being. Nor can a person genuinely renounce just because it is what another person wants or attempts to compel. No one can change the habitual center of personal energy of another person. James understood this acutely, especially when it came to stopping drinking. One can imagine that he witnessed his brother's attempts to stop when perhaps his brother did not have a genuine desire to quit. Or perhaps his brother did have the genuine desire, yet something drew him up short. His desire may have fallen short of a willingness to change. James's letters to family members about his brother's bouts of heavy drinking and periods of abstinence paint a vivid portrait of acute suffering and frustration.

Often people who are trying to quit using alcohol or other drugs hedge their bets or leave themselves an out, a layer of protection from complete abstinence. As James says

> A drunkard, or a morphine or cocaine maniac, offers himself to be cured. He appeals to a doctor to wean him from his enemy, but he dares not face blank abstinence....Everyone knows of cases of this incomplete and ineffective desire for reform....To really give up anything on which we have relied, to give up definitively, "for good and all" and forever, signifies one of those radical alterations of character....In it the inner man rolls over into an entirely different position of equilibrium, lives in a new center of energy from this time on, and the turning point and hinge of all such operations seems usually to involve the sincere acceptance of certain nakedness and destitutions (247).

Leaving an out, keeping some drugs in reserve "just in case," will not bring about the sort of transformation of character that one professes to want. One's actions and wishes are not congruent. Fully wanting inconsistent or even contradictory things is not uncommon with people struggling with addiction. The more divided a person's self is the more difficult it is for one's actions and wishes to be congruent. Some part of a struggling addict may really want to stop using and may even actively believe that he can, but other parts of the self have no desire to stop using. This internal division is a hallmark of addiction.

Furthermore, a person who tries to make such a big change but keeps an alleged safeguard in place may find himself moving further along the misery spectrum. Now he can claim that he has tried but failed. Perhaps he is the sort who cannot be cured. The consequences of his actions will continue to become more severe, and his life more miserable. He may move deeper into pathological melancholy.

Wishing and Willing

A person's attitude matters enormously. Does he wish to stop using or does he will to stop using? Willing and willingness need to be distinguished from desiring and wishing. The latter two can lead to incredible frustration and suffering. The former make possible great transformation.[19] James defines desire as wanting to feel, to have, or to do what presently is not felt, had, or done. Desires can be about anything. We desire material goods like cars, houses, a good meal, etc. We also desire immaterial goods such as relationships with others, acceptance, happiness, success, etc. The line between material and immaterial is not always hard and fast; one may physically desire another person in large part because of the love she has for him, her, or them. Physical desire may also increase love. Desire can increase when we want more than we presently have, and it can decrease when we no longer want what we have.

James's point about desire is there's always a gap between the wanting and the having. While in many cases the gap between wanting and having is traversable, the gap can increase when one is not attentive enough to both the strength and direction of desires and how those desires fit with what one already has. Paying more attention to what one wants rather than what one has may lead to growing dissatisfaction.

According to James, we wish when what we desire is accompanied by a sense that it cannot be attained or achieved. Wishing is defined by the sense that one cannot realize her desires. There are all sorts of reasons why someone's desires cannot be met and those reasons are not created equal. I wish I had won the $2 billion lottery drawing, but the odds were astronomically stacked against me. Wishes like this are not bad or dangerous and in fact can provide a welcome flight of fancy. Who wouldn't wish they'd have the opportunity to quit a job, pay off debt, help friends, etc.?

Problems begin when the reasons for something not being met or achieved have to do with me or what's in my control. I can wish until the cows come home that I will get the promotion at work. I can wish that tomorrow I will stop drinking or using drugs. I can wish to the point of pining for the partner of my dreams. Bigger problems follow when my wishes become wrapped in expectation. When expectation takes over, my focus becomes less on what I am doing and more on what I deserve. Putting on the "I deserve" lens renders us unable to see clearly the relationship between our inactions and our desires not being met. There's a good reason why many people in recovery define an expectation as a future resentment. That resentment is almost always directed at other people or more vaguely, "society." We fail to recognize that our inactions in many cases play an important role in our desires not being met.

James claims that we will when we believe we can achieve what we desire and we take appropriate actions. Willing necessarily requires action. This is what distinguishes wishing from willing. When a person wills, she recognizes that she is in a position to actualize something that she desires. In most cases, willing is a necessary condition for us to realize our desires. If I want the promotion, then I better work hard and finish my projects by the specified deadlines. If I want to stop drinking or using, then I need to take some action such as driving home a different way to avoid the liquor store or the place where I usually buy drugs.

Willing is a necessary but not sufficient condition to realize desires. Each of us has plenty of examples of acting to realize our desires in ways that fall short, go haywire, or bring about the exact opposite of what we want. That I will get a promotion is not simply a matter of my will alone. Too many other factors beyond my control are at play. There may be people who are far more qualified, or equally hard working, or the job description is not a match for my experience. Stopping drinking and using is not fully a matter of my will; I may need medications to curb cravings. I may need a much stronger support network than I presently have.

When I assume that realizing my desires is completely a matter of my will, frustration and overflowing resentment usually follow. If I am convinced that I am doing everything right and still I am not getting what I desire, then I might just keep pushing myself to do the same thing only harder every time. One definition of insanity is doing the same thing repeatedly but expecting different results. I may start to resent both those same results and other people who get different results from doing the same things I am.

When we will too much and try to force the world to bend or we will in the wrong direction—for example, willing to control something far beyond our control—we become unhappy. We can become miserable and susceptible to the world sickness discussed in chapter four. The solution is not to stop willing since that throws us back to the unhappiness that comes from unrealized wishes. Rather, we need to recognize what is in our control and what is not and then calibrate our expectations and act accordingly. We may need to be willing to act even or especially when we don't know what the results will be. In other words, we may need faith.

Acceptance and renunciation go together; they are flip sides of the same coin. Acceptance is the recognition that a situation is bigger than I alone can handle or comprehend. In the course of our daily living, we accept that many things are too big to handle alone. I cannot lift a 200-pound box without the assistance of another person or the help of a mechanical device. I accept that I cannot understand how to file my tax return without the aid of a certified public accountant. I accept that I cannot understand myself fully or accurately without the help of others. My friends give me a reality check and tell me, "No, you definitely don't want to do that if you also want this other thing to happen."

Acceptance involves activity and agency. Acceptance requires that my actions are responsive to changing realities as well as the recognition that my actions cannot guarantee the outcomes I want. Many external factors are beyond my control. What I can control is my attitude. This, too, involves a choice. By acting in deliberate and responsive ways, I may change both myself and my reality. This is what James realized in the throes of his panic fear. He not only needed to act differently but he also had to believe his actions would make a real difference.

We have no problem with acceptance in the vast majority of our lives. Yet, when it comes to quitting alcohol or drugs, we think that it should be within our control. Control is often about holding tightly to something—if I can just hold on tightly enough, I can retain control. Renunciation is, as I said above, about loosening that grip. Instead of clutching something familiar but harmful, I can reach toward something unfamiliar but helpful, or at least not harmful. In the process, I may become a little bit more tolerant of uncertainty.

Uncertainty can be terrifying, which is why people would rather stick with the devil they know than face the unknown. Each of us has an uncertainty threshold. Put another way, each person has his own point of tolerance for uncertainty. A person's uncertainty threshold is directly related to their faith. I am using "faith" in a much broader sense than belief in religious entities or a wider universal order. Faith can be about anything: I can have faith in institutions (I have faith the courts will uphold the rule of law), other people (I have faith this person will keep her promise), or myself (I have faith I will always do my best to be honest). The hallmark of faith, according to William James, is to believe in and act from possibility. Faith is a willingness to live in possibility and act on the maybes. It is the willingness to act as if what you do makes a difference.

Faith Makes Facts

James offers a full-throated defense of faith, especially religious faith, in two important lectures delivered in a short period and subsequently published together in 1896.[20] These are important to the views James later expresses in *Varieties*. "The Will to Believe" and "Is Life Worth Living?" are companion pieces arguing for a central role of faith in humans' lives. In "The Will to Believe," James describes faith as the adoption of a believing attitude toward spiritual matters even though our logical intellect may not be convinced. A person may voluntarily adopt an attitude of faith in spiritual matters. Faith is akin to a working hypothesis in the sense of being a big "what if." Faith is about possibilities and maybes. Faith runs through much of our daily life with science trafficking in it as much as any religion. Science and religion each rely on faith. What we now take to be the laws of physics were originally postulated as a series of hypothesis concerning gravity, relativity, and quantum mechanics, for example. Before they were proven, these hypotheses helped to build systems of knowledge. The Higgs Boson particle was postulated as part of a theory about the origin of mass in the universe more than 50 years ago. It wasn't until 2012 that this particle was revealed by the Large Haldron Collider. Scientists voluntarily adopted the hypothesis that such a particle existed and acted on it for decades before its existence was verified. If faith has a place in science, it certainly has a place in everyday life. It most surely has a place in the lives of people who struggle with addiction. Faith in the sense of being willing to act before any results are certified may play an enormous role in changing our relationships to addictive substances and behaviors.

In "The Will to Believe," James explores the various circumstances in which is a person entitled to hold a belief that has not been—and might never be—confirmed. When a person is forced to choose between two viable or live options and the stakes are momentous, one is entitled to believe even though the evidence is lacking. This is a situation in which there is no abstention and no avoidance. When life presents us with situations in which we must choose to act because the stakes are so high, we are justified to believe even though not all or even none of the evidence is in. We cannot wait for certainty and irrefutable arguments. We cannot wait for a bell of certainty to be ringing in our intellect. There's as much peril in waiting for that bell as there is in believing.[21]

Many people struggling with addiction are in just this sort of circumstance. Continuing to use seems a plausible or live option. Stopping using seems a really remote possibility, but it still has enough of a spark to be a live option. There's no avoiding this choice. To put it differently, making this choice has become part of the fabric of daily life. Each option is itself momentous. Continuing to use will lead to more harmful consequences to a person's material, social, and spiritual self—up to and including incapacitation and death. Stopping using will lead to life being altered in all sorts of ways. The choice may be a matter of life or death. In this circumstance, a person has a right to believe they can change behaviors. Despite all the evidence to the contrary including past failed attempts and doubts of friends or family, a person is entitled to believe that this time will be different.

Faith is the willingness or capacity to believe and act where doubt is still possible. Faith is what enables a person to continue to hold a belief where the evidence ends. Faith bridges that gap between belief and evidence and it can also help to build evidence. In "Is Life Worth Living?" James explores that most fundamental question many humans confront daily. Were we all healthy-minded, there would be no need to ask this question; it would be nonsensical. But for many, this question involves a forced and momentous choice between two live options. Continuing to live is a credible option, as is ceasing to live. There's no middle option and none with higher stakes. For those who are deeply pessimistic about their own worth or the worth of life itself, the question is a source of utter torment. Many incline toward a negative answer—life is not worth living. James has these people in mind throughout his lecture. People who answer no to that question are no strangers to him. James recognizes the darkness, pessimism, and melancholia because he himself struggled with them at different points in his life. No doubt James was asking himself about the worthiness of his own life. He was in a position of a forced and momentous decision between sinking even further or beginning to rise somehow. James had faith in free will—perhaps only a sliver of it—but it was enough to enliven further the hypothesis that his life was worth living. He chose to believe in free will and to believe his actions mattered. He didn't know what the results of his beliefs and actions would be in advance of his decision. He had to embrace the maybes and possibilities that were before him.

Maybes and possibilities are inescapable in human life. We must deal as much with possibilities as we do facts; they are unavoidable. Part of being human is negotiating and living with uncertainties at the same time that we generate certainties. James writes, "It is only by risking our persons from one hour to another that we live at all. And often enough our faith beforehand in an uncertified result is the only thing that makes the result come true." [22]

In "The Will to Believe," James offers an example to demonstrate the relationship between faith and a fact that preliminary faith may help to bring about. All of us at times wonder whether a certain person likes us or not.

Do you like me or not? Whether you do, James claims, is in part a consequence of my willingness to assume you do and consequently showing you friendliness and some degree of trust. James notes, "if I stand aloof and refuse to budge an inch until I have objective evidence … ten to one your liking never comes."[23] There's no bell of intellectual certainty to ring in this matter. My previous faith in your liking me, even if it is the most fragile and tentative, contributes to the fact you do like me.

In "Is Life Worth Living?" James asks his listeners and readers to imagine they have climbed a mountain and have landed in a treacherous spot where the only escape is a terrible leap. A person who believes he can make the leap fortifies himself and his feet. When he doubts and mistrusts, he may change his actions. He may hesitate, worry about failure, and in despair, fall into the abyss.[24] Doubt and mistrust, like faith, are living attitudes that are woven right into our actions. Faith in making the leap is what helps to make the leap.

James concludes his discussion about the worth of life by arguing that life feels like a real fight and that each of us is part of the fight. We don't know if there is any afterlife or heavenly reward; those are uncertified results. We have the here and now. James counsels us in that essay, "Be not afraid of life. Believe that life is worth living, and your belief will help create the fact."[25] To have faith is to grab a hold of a maybe.

Living on a Maybe of Recovery

People struggling with addiction are standing in a treacherous spot too. A person who is eager to escape a life in which he is actively addicted still has some hope. The nature of this hope is crucial. Is it a hope that is all about wishing or is it a hope paired with willing? Hope paired with willing is a first cousin to faith. What kinds of actions are people willing to take to get themselves out of the present incompleteness and wrongness of their lives? Our actions help to enliven the hypothesis that we can act differently. We face a forced and momentous choice between the live options of continuing to use and changing our use. For some of us, the severity of our use makes this question of whether to continue or change our use a version of James's question. It is a matter of life or death.

For others whose addictions haven't progressed as far, the choice is still pressing. What kind of maybe or possibility might be available to a person grappling with this question? What is a possibility will be relative to each particular person in much the same way the liveness of a hypothesis is. For one person, it may be something as simple as forming a belief that life doesn't have to be this way. Or perhaps there is something—anything—better than this way of living. Someone else might see possibility for himself by looking at someone else who used as much or as dangerously as he did but no longer does. A person who tends to trust medical authorities might say something to her physician in the belief he may be able to help. Another may believe a minister might be able to help. One may say to himself that maybe he can refuse the next drink or hit. Someone else thinks it may be possible to cut down her use. Maybe he will be able to wean himself off his addictive substances or behaviors. Four hours not using may seem impossible but one hour might be possible. He tries for an hour. Perhaps he fails the first seven times. While these attempts might be seen as an indicator of the severity of a person's Substance Use Disorder, they may also be indications that someone is willing to do things differently. He manages to get an hour. His belief that he could do it contributes to his doing it. For him, it is an incredible achievement. Then he does it for several hours. The more he doesn't drink, the more he comes to believe that he can do it for twenty-four hours. All the evidence is against him on this count, but he cannot afford to wait. Then he does it. Then perhaps he can do it for 25 hours. His faith that he will be able not to use continues to grow and he acts from that faith. He conjures into reality both his faith and the fact that he does not drink. These facts support his faith, which in turn will help him to make new facts about his use. Here, too, there is no guarantee or certified result. A person has a better chance of not using if he has faith—understood as willingness to live in the possibility—that he can stop using.

This is a very different account from a view of faith that posits that a divine being is operative and somehow keeping a person from drinking or using. Many people do believe in such a being, making it a live option for them. The belief works for them. The importance of a belief goes beyond its particular content and includes what the belief brings about or produces. How does faith in something bring about actions that transform a person? James knew that many objected to his view that a person is justified or has a right to believe in something before all the evidence is gathered. Scientists and other philosophers were contemptuous of this view, but James forged ahead by showing examples when faith is as much a part of the scientific process as verification. He called out his critics for whom religious hypotheses were dead for applying "some patent superstition" to the concept of faith and religion.[26] James was ever so careful not to pack the concept of religious or spiritual with content that reflects a particular faith tradition or privileges one faith tradition over another. For James, the object of faith can be a something More, a consciousness greater than my own, a better self, moral and civic principles, or even humanity. The thinnest of beliefs in any of these may be more than enough to begin a remarkable transformation of life. Coming to identify, hold, and then act on these beliefs is part of a conversion.

Faith is a willingness to live possibilities in order to make new facts. These facts then support our faith and that openness to possibilities. The changes faith brings about may be incremental or immediate depending on the type of conversion one experiences. The results of these changes are significant. They may lead a person to embrace her life with a resounding Yes. She becomes able to reap the fruit of the spiritual tree.

Chapter Seven
Fruits of the Spiritual Tree

The transition from tenseness, self-responsibility, and worry to equanimity, receptivity, and peace is the most wonderful of all those shiftings of our inner equilibrium, those changes of the personal centre of energy.

WILLIAM JAMES

Much of the discussion about conversions has focused on the transformation of the habitual center of personal energy. A person becomes a new person, which does not mean disowning the past but rather standing in a new relationship to it and making a more intentional course for the future. The people who most need transformation are those,

> whose existence is little more than a series of zigzags, as now one tendency and now another gets the upper hand. Their spirit wars with their flesh, they wish for incompatibles, wayward impulses interrupt their most deliberate plans, and their lives are one long drama of repentance and of effort to repair misdemeanors and mistakes (134).

This is an accurate way to describe most addicts. We are riddled with inconsistencies and contradictions. We will go to any length to maintain the impossible. When we cannot, some of us will feel like failures while others will blame everyone and everything in sight. We will rarely find peace, or our peace will be with our use and will be both false and fleeting. Transformation and regeneration bring about unification by righting the imbalances and stopping the chaos, incongruence, and inconsistencies. Nothing is more wearying than that dramatic cycle of repentance and attempts at repair. When a person is transformed, they will stop having that drama be the story of their life. That is not to say that they will not need to apologize and repair when they have done something wrong, but it won't have the same crazy-making drama.

There is an avalanche of thoughts and feelings following on the heels of a conversion, especially of the sudden sort. These feelings are amplified when a person believes in a supernatural God, as did Hadley, Alline, and the young Oxford graduate. While Bill Wilson professed to having no belief in God, he had a deep familiarity with Christian theology. Among the changes a person experiences is a sense of higher control or a higher controlling agency. Alline, Hadley, and the young graduate each believed God had done something to him, relieving him from the source of his suffering. Each expressed a sense of God's having made a change in him, which became a new course for living. Conversions are also followed by states of assurance, in which worries dissolve and a sense of peace follows. Even if all the external conditions of life remain the same, a person comes to have a newfound willingness to meet the world. The assurance may be a consequence of a relief in no longer having to worry so much about controlling the uncontrollable.

There is also a strong sense, James claims, that the newly converted person is able to perceive new truths that he had not known before. Both Alline and the young graduate suddenly understood familiar Bible passages in new ways. This new knowledge may also be self-knowledge about what a person can or cannot do on her own with respect to alcohol and other drugs. It may also be self-knowledge about a person's relations to others and her place in the world. This self-knowledge is the antidote to self-deception.

The newly converted experience the world as different. Moreover, it isn't just that the person changes; the world may change. The world is brighter, clearer, and more vibrant. This beauty and newness of the world combined with the sense that a person has transformed may provide a kind of ecstasy, exaltation, or rapture (190-193). The root of "ecstasy," is displacement or trance, which means one is in a different state of awareness. The rational part of the consciousness may be somewhat muted or even eclipsed by elements of the subconscious and transmarginal regions. Being in an ecstatic state may result in hallucinations or visions. This was Bill Wilson's worry after his experience in the Towns Hospital. Was he going crazy imagining a gust of spirit and no longer desiring to drink?

Individually and taken as a package, these thoughts and feelings can be profoundly disorienting. Alline was so worried he might lose his newfound beliefs that he was afraid to fall asleep lest they disappear. The young Oxford graduate was so exhilarated his first day that he heralded it all around town. By the next day, he was splitting hairs about not having promised God he would not drink. Not having made that promise, he drank heavily. In backsliding as he did, he didn't lose it all. He may not have lost anything and even gained something. Even having a short twenty-four hours as the graduate did shows a person "the high water mark of his spiritual capacity" (200). Where before a person might have claimed to possess no spiritual capacity, the young graduate experienced some of his, inchoate though it was. That experience may serve as a positive ideal in continuing to change.

Expansiveness and our Habitual
Centers of Personal Energy

The unification that a person achieves as she is spiritually transformed results in what James calls Saintliness. A person who is saintly has a "character for which spiritual emotions are the habitual center of personal energy" (211). The words "saintly" and "saintliness" are likely to be off-putting to many, since these terms are often used in a Christian context. In order to avoid those connotations, I propose to substitute with the terms "expansively" and "expansiveness." These terms owe no allegiance to any particular religious, ethical, or philosophical approach.

Expansiveness involves a person extending outward to something More or greater than her previously embattled self. A person may also reach inward to a better self. This expansiveness enables a person to begin to say yes to life.

People who become expansive as a result of a conversion and have undergone a shift in their habitual center of personal energy will experience life in a new way because they are new people. Altering a habitual center of personal energy is reflected in all dimensions of the self. A person's material, social, and spiritual selves have changed in the process of unification. Her body may be radically altered as it adapts to the absence of particular substances and their effects. She may have lost or gained a great deal of weight. Her face may bear the marks of her use. Her family is also part of her material self. Some family members may race to embrace her lovingly and fully while others maintain a safe distance. Material goods she prized most highly may be lost forever. Other goods she previously prized lose their luster. Either the goods themselves or their loss may feel a burden. She might even experience a sense of relief at working so hard for so long to maintain the appearance of normalcy.

A person's social selves change significantly when she changes her relationship to alcohol and other drugs. She may rekindle friendships and other relationships she had lost as a consequence of her use. At the same time, she may prune relationships that keep her tethered to her using days. She will have as many social selves as there are individuals who recognize and carry an image of her in their minds, as James notes. She may need to accept and navigate relationships where she is viewed negatively. If she has burned bridges personally and professionally, others may continue to view her as unreliable or unprofessional. To others, especially those who have only known her since she stopped using, she may be seen as competent, hardworking, and dedicated to making significant changes in her life. Others may see her as an inspiration and a source of insight and wisdom even as she worries about being exposed as a fraud. Since our social selves are hierarchical—meaning that some of them are more important than others—she may face the daunting challenge of reordering them in light of her new priorities and commitments. Part of that reordering may take the form of not caring, or at least not caring as much, about what other people think of her. She may come to realize that, but for a few core relationships in her life, it really isn't her business or concern what others think of her.

A person's spiritual self will also undergo seismic changes. In our using days, especially if our use had progressed to a moderate or severe Substance Use Disorder or into the most bleak stages of World Sickness, we often misdirected and misfired our intellectual and emotional energies. For many, our lives were dramas of offense, apology, repair, and re-offense. Our intellectual interests and capacities may have shrunk, and our emotional palettes may have dulled as we grew numb to pleasures and joys. Losing these opened up the space for fear and anxiety to take root and flourish. In the worst stages of World Sickness, only the abject fear remains; there is no counterbalance. After a conversion as the internal fog starts to lift, a person may need to reignite her intellectual abilities and interests and channel them in more appropriate and fruitful directions. Most importantly, she must direct her attention and effort toward figuring out how to live without addictive substances and behaviors. This is a steep learning curve littered with missteps and mistakes. A person's making mistakes is to be expected. What she does after making them is what matters. Like the young Oxford graduate, even in 24 hours she may see the high-water mark of her spiritual capacity.

There's no one characteristic common to all people who are newly converted for the simple reason that each person's expansiveness comes from, reflects, and augments that person's individuality. However, it is still possible to offer a composite sketch of four features of the inner lives of transformed people. These features will shape the present and future courses of their lives.

Four Features of Transformation

The first feature of the inner lives of the converted is a sense of being in a world wider than one's self and selfish interest. No one person is the totality of the universe. That realization prompts many to develop the conviction that there is an Ideal Power within that wider universe (211). The language of Ideal Power may be particularly troublesome to many in the context of addiction and recovery. James says this power in Christian thought is always personified as God. But, it may also be "abstract moral ideals, civic or patriotic utopias, or inner visions of holiness or rightness may also be felt as the true lords and enlargers of our life" (211). He also says in a footnote, and this is an important acknowledgement of what can be called secular humanism, that "the enthusiasm of humanity" leads to a life that appears indistinguishable from Christian saintliness (211 footnote).

For people who have been betrayed at every turn and believe that there are all and only bad and untrustworthy people in the world, to entertain the idea that there are some good people is a remarkable achievement. Seeing people help others and seeing people willing to ask and accept help may have been impossible for people who had progressed far along the spectrum of world sickness. Catching a glimpse of others or your own self as good, decent, and worthy can be an ideal power that leads to the conviction you are not alone anymore.

The second feature of the inner lives of transformed people is a sense of a friendly continuity of this power with our own lives. This friendliness makes a person willing to surrender to that power in the ways discussed in the previous chapter. Our awareness of what James calls this "higher and friendly Power" is the most important. It is the fundamental feature of a spiritual life. When and how do we become aware of this Higher or Ideal Power? To show one of the many different ways this Power is experienced by people, James quotes Thoreau, who wrote about living in Walden Pond for an extended period of time. Admittedly Thoreau got lonely at times, but then one day standing in the rain,

> I was sensible of such sweet and beneficent society in nature, in the very patterning of the drops, and in every sight and sound around my house, an infinite and unaccountable friendliness all at once, like an atmosphere, sustaining me, as made the fancied advantages of human neighborhood insignificant, and I have never thought of them since. Every little pine needle expanded and swelled with sympathy and befriended me. I was so distinctly made aware of the presence of something kindred to me, that I thought no place could ever be strange to me again (quoted 213).

This is a very different understanding of Ideal Power from a personified deity. At Walden, Thoreau becomes aware of not being alone; he was in the company of all of nature. Nature and he are kindred spirits, making a connection that extends beyond Walden Pond to the rest of the world. No part of nature is foreign to him since he himself is a part of nature. Put differently, Thoreau shares a communion with all that Nature is. There is so much more to life than his own self-interests and all the alleged advantages that human society offers. Thoreau opens himself to both the external and internal possibilities that nature offers.

Thoreau sees himself as being part of nature, no less or more so than the pine needle. He experiences "friendly continuity" with nature. In accepting that there are certain conditions in nature that cannot be thwarted (no one can control the rain or the winds), one can renounce the illusion of control. One shows an acceptance of the power of the weather by taking shelter or riding out a storm. Good sailors know the importance of not sailing too close to the wind; when one does, she assumes that she can control conditions far beyond anyone's control. Renouncing is akin to tacking; one recognizes that she cannot just sail straight into the wind. She needs to be open to the possibility of moving the sails, changing directions, and perhaps taking a sail down or putting up another. Surrendering to the conditions of the wind is not passive. On the contrary, surrendering means she acts in different ways that increase possibilities rather than foreclosing them. This is what James means when he writes about the newly converted or unified person willingly surrendering control to a greater power. It isn't that a deity will act for or on a person. Rather, a person is willing and able to act differently in ways that are responsive to the conditions.

Reaching or expanding outward to something More makes it more difficult to be selfish and only self-regarding. A person notices more in the world to or for which she feels connection and responsibility. As a person expands outward to others and inward to herself, the loneliness and isolation that are so common to lives of active addiction lessen. The irony, as Alline noticed about his days of carousing and debauchery, is that one can be the chief instigator of fun and surrounded by people yet feel devastatingly alone. That isolation can be soul crushing. Expansiveness is the antidote to the isolation.

The third feature of a transformed person's inner life is a sense of freedom and elation that follows from the melting of "outlines of the confining selfhood." This freedom is immeasurable. All those views and beliefs about how a person should be or what sort of interests or concerns should matter tend to shackle a person. Letting go of all those expectations, whether foisted upon us by others or imposed on ourselves, is liberating. Those expectations may make a person unwilling to say yes to anything that challenges others' views of us or shakes our own self-perception. A person may also disavow parts of herself in order to maintain a façade or to garner approval from others. Each of us can confine our own self as much as others can confine us. Freed from all these self- and other-imposed expectations, a person can lift her eyes to a broader horizon and perceive new possibilities.

Work in recovery—both early and late—requires coming to recognize the many ways others confine us and we confine ourselves. Some of those confines may be very familiar—they may even be all we have known—and therefore they are comfortable in a certain way. Some may even have brought us real benefit. As we dissolve these confines, we feel as if we are perceiving new truths even as we look at old familiar facts. We achieve a remarkable degree of self-knowledge when we can intentionally undo those confines. Some of those confines will be ripped out while others will be gently unstitched in a very intentional and cautious way. We begin a new relationship to our self. In seeing how our material, social, and spiritual selves have been in the past, we are able to imagine and actualize new selves in the future.

Having tamped down the more selfish inclinations and affections, there is now more room for those positive affections that reach out to others and inward to one's self. This is the fourth characteristic of converted and expansive people. By negotiating a cease fire between warring factions or identities, a person has the opportunity to be more integrated and unified. Integration will be a matter of degrees relative to each person. A cease fire may be the highest degree of unification one person can achieve while another may become close to seamlessly integrated. Put another way, there will always be some divisions within each person, but the degree or depth of those divisions decrease after a conversion. Partly the unification is a consequence of the newly acquired expansive orientation. The expansiveness creates a new depth within a person at the same time that it extends to other people and nature, as Thoreau described. Embodying that more expansive attitude creates possibilities. Where before possibilities may have been terrifying because each one might lead to failure, now new possibilities could mean more happiness if only one says yes to them. Possibilities may become opportunities to become even more expansive.

Transformations to Lives of Recovery

How does a person's life look who has undergone a transformation or regeneration of the sort that becomes part of a life of sobriety? Most importantly, a person is no longer a divided soul in the ways he was when drinking or using. He comes to embody a harmony, congruence, and consistency that he could not when drinking or using. The unification of self that is brought about in the process of conversion has several important characteristics. Each one is crucial, but their combination is vital. James offers three of these characteristics: firmness, stability, and equilibrium. Each is a proper balance between opposite extremes. One extreme involves too much of a quality and the other too little of a quality. A person who is unified will have these virtues and will therefore have the capacity and compassion to respond as opposed to merely react in appropriate ways. A person still in the throes of an active addiction usually will fall on either the excess or deficiency side.

A person who is unified has a certain firmness of mind and character. That is to say, she is someone who has clear beliefs and attitudes and acts from them. She acts according to the principles she holds most closely and acts in ways that affirm who she is as a person. However, she can adapt and is open to questioning herself and beliefs when presented with opportunities, especially when they enable her to learn and grow. The person who is completely set in her beliefs and under no circumstances will question herself or allow others to question her has too much firmness that has hardened into rigidity. Contrasted with her is the person who makes decisions on whims and seems to have no rhyme or reason for why she does things.

Stability is the second virtue of unification. Consider a house. In some construction locations, it would be ill advised not to have a foundation. In other locations, a foundation is not possible. In any construction, stability comes from several features and depends on available building materials. Some walls are load bearing. Some beams carry weight. Stability in a house is a combination of factors, and a good builder understands the relationships between these and attends to each individually but never loses sight of the whole. The same is true with a person's character. Stability in character comes from our relationships with our family and friends and how these intersect with our histories, commitments, core beliefs, goals, and dreams. The person who has stability in excess perhaps runs the risk of not being open to new experience because it might introduce a little uncertainty or change. She preserves the stability because it is known and familiar and is closed off from possibility. She says no too often and quickly. On the other hand, the person who lacks stability has no steady and safe relationships to which she can turn. She lives with an abiding uncertainty because there are no relationships that can help her to bear burdens. She is the classic zigzagger saying yes to whatever catches her fancy at the moment.

The third characteristic of a unified person is equilibrium. Equilibrium is balance; it is a state of rest that results from equal opposing forces. With respect to mental and emotional states, it is sometimes called equanimity or calm. Maintaining balance is crucial not just when walking a high wire but in every aspect of living. Think of standing while on a boat in choppy waters. Oftentimes one has to shift one's feet and weight to keep from falling over.

Shifting weight can be gradual but sometimes one needs to really throw oneself in the other direction. Having good equilibrium means being able to make adjustments needed to stay balanced in the face of factors beyond your control. Some adjustments can be done with little conscious thought. At other times, one needs to be very intentional about how one shifts the balance lest one go too far in the opposite direction. The person with too much equilibrium will never allow anything to alter even slightly their balance. It is as if she has scales on the table and she carefully rearranges the items on each side, but will never let one item fall off or move over to the other side. Her scales are in a state of nearly total rest. The person with no equilibrium is the person who continues standing upright in the boat in choppy water, getting knocked all around and perhaps falling on other persons. She can never come to a state of rest because every pull in whatever direction will overpower her.

An active addict's life lacks firmness, stability, and equilibrium. It is a life of zigzags and warring wants and needs. It is a life of big drama, never-ending repentance, and attempts to repair misdemeanors and mistakes. With addicts, the pendulum can swing wildly back and forth between attempts to control and wild binges. Or it may be between genuine regret and total and willful defiance. The point is that with these swings, there is no balance. Addicts suffer from a malady that is indicative of the world sickness discussed in chapter four.

Stopping the Whiplash

A transformed person is a new person as James so richly describes. But this is not to say that they have left their past behind, but rather they stand in a different relationship to it. This is a matter of the kind of stability they create by keeping their relationships in good order. A twice-born person is different from others in terms of how they live and act in the world. They are a person capable of a wide range of emotions, able to admit mistakes, make amends, and give credit where credit is due.

A person's life will be transformed in ways that are overt and subtle, sudden and gradual. Some of these changes will not be noticeable until someone else points them out. At times it will feel as though change has happened over night while other times it feels as if change will never happen. But what does happen in the process of transformation?

> That whole raft of cowardly obstructions, which in tame persons and dull moods are sovereign impediments to actions, sink away at once. Our conventionality, our shyness, laziness, and stinginess, our demands for precedent and permission, for guarantee and surety, our small suspicions, timidities, despairs, where are they now? Severed like cobwebs, broken like bubbles in the sky (207).

When one thinks everything should be about him and his only concern is himself, he will end up miserable and exhausted. Whatever glimpses of happiness he might catch, happiness will always be at risk; something will always come along and present challenges. Any slight difficulty will be blown out of proportion and seen as an egregious assault on wellbeing. The selfish person is often governed by fear and fear-thought; what starts as a plausible and understandable fear about one thing morphs into a super-spreading event. When one undergoes a spiritual transformation and begins to realize that there is so much more to the world and living than just you, it may first come as something of a shock, then a relief, and finally a source of great happiness. A good person who helps another is often happy and grateful that he has the opportunity to do so. Where there is no advantage to be gained in helping another yet the reasons for doing so are fairly clear, the rewards are many. Selfish concerns choke us and keep us clutching to anything we can find. Selfless concerns open us to possibility and expand our lives, helping us let go of old concerns.

When we have stopped careening around in zigzag patterns and our impulses no longer have sovereignty over us, then we are much better positioned to take life as it comes to us. Often times we rush into situations hoping to make the preemptive strike or to gain control. When we are transformed and the previously warring factions within us are unified, we gain a quiet, well-grounded confidence about our abilities to be in the world harmoniously, even when things are in upheaval. This is another way of saying that transformed and regenerated people recalibrate their misery thresholds. Instead of remaining on, finding comfort in, and believing there is no alternative to the darker side of life, people may be willing to believe there are alternatives. That belief may help to make those alternatives attainable. A person may have some faith that life can be different. It may be a smidgen less miserable, a lot less miserable but still not good, or perhaps even good. Whereas before fear—of failing, disappointing others, being found out, and relapsing—was the primary motive, now there's room for other motives.

Of course, this is not to say that converted people are never miserable and never struggle. Most likely they will do both at different times. But they will know another way of being in the world and will be reminded of how life can be when spiritual affections are the habitual center of their personal energy. They have seen a higher water mark for their spiritual lives. People who have spiritual impulses as the center of their habitual center of personal energy will burn with an acute fever.

Chapter Eight
Living with the Acute Fever

We all have moments when the universal life seems to wrap us round with friendliness.

WILLIAM JAMES

The acute fever of those who live with spiritual matters at the habitual center of their personal energy caught William James' attention. In the stories of Christian saints, that acute fever often took the form of extreme acts of denial and self-inflicted harm. While these stories are fascinating in many ways, people who undergo a spiritual conversion typically do not engage in such flamboyant practices. Rather, it is often impossible to tell at first glance who does have spiritual matters at the center of their personal energy from those who do not. There is no equivalent of a sack cloth, merit badges, or medals to distinguish those who have been transformed. Often there is serenity or peacefulness. But that serenity, paradoxical as it may seem, burns as an acute fever to those who have been transformed or regenerated.

People in recovery live with an acute fever. Being in recovery, however, doesn't entail that people no longer make mistakes, suffer in myriad ways, and even long for parts of themselves from their using days. People may still have cravings though the character of cravings changes over time. Nothing can inoculate against craving, suffering, and making mistakes, but the fruits of the spiritual tree better position people to navigate the world in safer and more sustainable ways.

This chapter explores some of the ways that people in recovery may burn with an acute fever. I will go beyond what James says on the matter though I hope James would regard me as a fellow traveler. I'll explore why and how some may still be susceptible to craving, struggle with self-knowledge and self-forgiveness, require flexibility in their recovery, and actively choose gratitude over grievance. Choosing gratitude over grievance is the greatest way to say Yes to life.

The Siren Call of Alcohol and Drugs

In much of the addiction literature, cravings appear to be a tsunami of desire correlated with familiar places and associated with past usage. Cravings just rise up unbidden and feel overwhelming. Cravings are like a mugging. This "cravings as mugging" picture accurately describes the cravings that some experience, especially those who still actively use or are recently sober.

However, this picture of cravings as mugging is not emblematic of all craving. We've been captivated by this picture, which carries an accompanying assumption that cravings *must* always be this way. The danger with this picture and its embedded assumption is that we may be unable to recognize other forms of craving. There needs to be more nuanced accounts of craving in the context of addiction. Different drugs and addictive behaviors affect the brain and the body in different ways. Cravings will not be experienced in identical ways because they are not just one thing, nor are they one dimension. They may be physical, cognitive, emotional, or spiritual. If we think that cravings are all and only big physiological/chemical tsunamis that knock us over, we will not recognize other forms of cravings. Additionally, cravings may be experienced differently depending on how long one has been in recovery or remission.

I submit there is another form of craving, one that is more akin to the confidence con or what is sometimes called the long con. A long con takes time to develop and often the best "marks" are those who believe themselves to be too smart/sophisticated/experienced to ever be duped. The con man earns the trust of the mark and then is in the best position to swindle or dupe. People with long term sobriety may be more susceptible to this form of craving precisely because they believe they are beyond craving or would recognize the tsunami if it came crashing down on them. A person undergoing a conversion away from addictive substances and behaviors shifts her habitual center of personal energy. Her selves—material, social, and spiritual—have changed and continue to do so in recovery.

Unsurprisingly, as her selves change, the character of her cravings changes as well. The danger is not recognizing this.

To understand the dynamics of both forms of craving (mugging and long con), I turn to the Sirens of ancient Greek mythology. The Sirens were half-woman/half bird creatures who lived on an island and lured sailors to their death with song. Enchanted not just by their voices but the beautiful lyrics, sailors would tack toward the coast and crash their vessels on the rocky shoals. They might drown or starve to death on the island because they were too captivated to gather food. The Sirens represent not just temptation but craving with deadly consequences. This classic Greek myth is illuminating for understanding the call that drugs, alcohol, and other addictive behaviors have for people who are in some stage of recovery.

In the stories of the Sirens, winds that had been favorable for sailing would suddenly fall calm when a ship neared the island. There would be no choice but to row past it. With no sound in the sails, an eerie silence settled over the water. And then the Sirens would start to sing. Only twice did a ship successfully pass the island. The first was Jason and the Argonauts who were returning from a heroic adventure to secure the Golden Fleece. Orpheus, the world's most accomplished musician, played such beautiful music with his lyre that the sailors paid more attention to it than the Sirens' song and so safely passed the island. The second was Odysseus and his men returning home after ten years fighting in Troy. Odysseus ordered his sailors to plug their ears with wax and tie him to the mast with the strict instructions to bind him more tightly should he order them to untie him. Once out of earshot, the men are free from the lure of the Sirens' song.

What was so irresistible about their song and how does this connect to cravings? The Sirens knew who was on the ships. They called to Odysseus with a song meant just for him. It was a song about heroism, the most important virtue in a warrior culture. It is a song about a way of life (being a hero) and how one understands or sees oneself. Great heroes died in the Trojan War, and now these warriors are returning home. Is there anything heroic in returning home? The Sirens called to Odysseus,

> Come hither, as thou farest, renowned Odys-
> seus, great glory of the Achaeans; stay thy ship
> that thou mayest listen to the voice of us two.
> For never yet has any man rowed past this isle
> in his black ship until he has heard the sweet
> voice from our lips. Nay, he has joy of it, and
> goes his way a wiser man. For we know all the
> toils that in wide Troy the Argives and Trojans
> endured through the will of the gods, and we
> know all things that come to pass upon the
> fruitful earth![27]

The song weaves together all the best dimensions of Odysseus's material, social, and spiritual selves with promises of a lasting heroic legacy and a future of wealth and power.

Who wouldn't want to move a little closer to hear a song that is all about you and that shows you to be the person you really want to be? Or even more strongly, the person you need to be? That's craving, deep craving. The Sirens' song shows us that the craving isn't only for a chemical and its effects but for a way of life and of seeing ourselves in certain ways.

Navigating the Temptations

Much of the advice to people who are newly sober or trying to abstain is to avoid situations where there will be temptations. This is akin to saying to the sailors, "stay as far away as possible from the island where those bird ladies are. Find another route home." This is very good advice. If you avoid the temptations, you avoid setting off cravings that may lead you to use.

If you can't find another route and you have to sail past that island of drugs and alcohol (if a family member continues to use, for example), is there an equivalent of Orpheus's music to drown out their call? Are there other ways to direct your focus or keep your attention on something else? Some people substitute one substance or behavior for another. Some people quit drinking but start smoking cigarettes. Others switch to marijuana. Some even say that they will quit smoking after they get an addiction under control. And yes, many do just that. However, there's potential for trouble here, especially if "healthier" really means "not as unhealthy." Diversion from one addiction may result in troubling consequences.

The equivalent of being tied to the mast is having a strong network of people who help to keep you in place. Those who help others go through withdrawal are most like Odysseus's sailors. To witness such physical and emotional brutality is itself brutal. So, too, is resisting the withdrawal sufferer's pleas and cries. Short of that extreme situation, the right friends, family, professionals, and other sources of support can create a durable netting that keeps a person in place. The netting can loosen over time as a person has longer sobriety or has sharply reduced their harmful use.

What does this myth tell us about long con cravings? A person with long term sobriety may come to believe that he is already beyond temptation; he's successfully sailed past the island. This confidence may make him an easy mark. The song appeals both to the past and the future; noticeably absent is the present. The danger of the song is its deeply personal nature. Long con cravings appeal to a past seen through rose colored glasses; we humans tend to rewrite past events or even past versions of ourselves over time. In some ways, we miss the *person* we imagine ourselves to have been. We miss an imaginary life where the consequences of our use weren't all that bad—we were still able to be a good partner/son/daughter/parent/friend, and our lives weren't defined by a catalogue of obligations and responsibilities. Our imagined past self starts to feel more real than our actual present self.

The Sirens' song also appeals to an imaginary future that is just as deeply personal as the nostalgic remembrances. If we have rose-tinted glasses looking at our past, we see our futures with sky-blue tinted glasses. We imagine a future that fulfills all of our hopes, dreams, and aspirations that also includes "normal" use of alcohol, drugs, or behaviors. We will be a good partner/son/daughter/parent/friend, the life of the party, and a success. We will be everything we ever hoped to be. When our expectations are not met or our imaginings fail to become realities, we may feel especially resentful and wronged. We may see other people and events as the cause of our disappointments rather than ourselves.

What of the present, when the winds calm and you find yourself having to row past the island? The deep longings or cravings are most often a response to something in a person's life. The important part is figuring out what that something is. Three other considerations are just as important. The first is maintaining an attitude of genuine humility toward one's sobriety. Never take it for granted. Sobriety isn't a given. The second is maintaining a healthy skepticism about both memories of our past selves and imaginings of our futures. The third consideration is coming to know ourselves in genuine ways. Self-knowledge is very much a fruit of the spiritual tree.

For the ancient Greeks, seeking self-knowledge was one of the most valuable pursuits a man could undertake. "Know thyself" was inscribed on the Temple at Delphi, the most important shrine in classical Greece where people came here to seek knowledge of the future from Phythia, the priestess of Apollo. The questions might range from when a farmer should plant a crop to when a king should declare war. The answers Pythia gave were often cryptic and subject to multiple interpretations. She gave answers but those answers required work to understand. It might seem odd to consider coming to know yourself as work. It's not just work; it is very hard work.

Knowing How to Belong to Yourself

It seems that knowing ourselves or knowing how to belong to ourselves should be easy. After all, each of us is an expert on their own experiences with unique access to their own thoughts, beliefs, and feelings. The expectation is that I should know all the material, social, and spiritual selves that constitute me. A common mistake is to assume that there is nothing more easily known than oneself. Knowing oneself is perhaps so difficult because we are simultaneously the inquirer and the object studied. It is difficult to get an accurate perspective. It is similar to a middle-aged person who can no longer see things up close without taking off the glasses she needs to see distant objects. Despite the difficulties in seeing oneself (literally and metaphorically), one must learn to do so.

Self-knowledge is not a luxury but rather a necessity. Not having self-knowledge can lead to harmful or even catastrophic consequences. So how might each of us come to know herself? The Oracle of Delphi has more to offer us about self-knowledge. Among numerous other inscriptions at the temple, two are especially important. The first is "Nothing in Excess." The second is "Surety, then calamity" or, alternatively, "A pledge then ruin." Putting these maxims together is important for understanding what it means to belong to oneself, which is an important part of living with an acute fever in recovery.

What does it mean to take nothing in excess? People in recovery are familiar with excess. A message in early recovery is that nothing is more important than your recovery.

There is something true about this, but there's a possibility that self-concern becomes self-absorption. Being too self-absorbed will be a barrier to genuine self-knowledge. Self-absorption and self-knowledge are "near enemies," which means that the unhelpful one (self-absorption) masquerades as the helpful one (self-knowledge). If you fail to see that who you are includes what you do, with whom you do those things, and the core identities you have (sister, brother, worker, citizen), then you end up with a very skewed view of yourself. In some ways, you may have too much trust in your capacity to know yourself, which renders you incapable of seeing or hearing how other people experience you. Each of us can learn an enormous amount from understanding how others experience us. Where there is divergence in how I see myself and how others see me, that should indicate that something is amiss and requires further examination.

The recommendation to guard against surety or certainty because it can be a precursor to trouble is important in recovery. The false certainty can be about oneself or about others and their views. Often the two are related. A person may be falsely certain about who they believe themselves to be. This is an interesting instance of dogmatism; a person believes they already know everything there is to know about themselves. Such a person may believe it impossible to surprise themselves. They also tend to believe that no one else has anything interesting to teach them about themselves. Their feedback loop will be closed, which may produce a host of problems including a version of the self-absorption mentioned above.

Each of us internalizes wholesale beliefs, values, and judgments about the way the world is and should be. This internalization is part of how we mature and come to see ourselves in the world. But if we take these as absolute certainties and never question them, we may become rigid in our understanding of the world, our place in it, and who each of us is as an individual. But this may prove to be very damaging because we end up belonging more to those beliefs and others who hold them than we belong to ourselves. We may give far too much power to others to define us, which returns us to the maxim, "nothing in excess."

All three maxims point to a tension about how much to trust yourself and how much to trust others. Most of us live that tension every day. Crucial for coming to belong to oneself is knowing which of those inherited beliefs, values, and judgments to reject because they do not fit us or they cost too much to continue holding. At times we may be willing to go to extremes to hold onto beliefs even as all the facts buck against them. At other times, we may too easily give up beliefs and values we know to be good and right for us. Not just recognizing, but also living this tension is an important step in knowing how to belong to yourself.

We are, at all times, involved in what the philosopher Montaigne (whom James read and admired) describes as the most important undertaking. He writes, "The glorious masterpiece of man is to live to purpose. All other things: to reign, to lay up treasure, to build, are but little appendices and props."[28] This masterpiece is created only with right intention and attention, which necessarily requires knowing how to belong to oneself. In recovery, each of us has the opportunity to create that masterpiece.

In coming to belong to oneself, a person gains a better perspective on why she did what she did and how many of her choices were made between rocks and hard places. She may have undertaken a moral inventory. A comprehensive moral inventory includes not only past transgressions but also past achievements. The inventory looks back to the past in order to have a better perspective on the future. There is much to be gained in these inventories and where appropriate, making amends to other people. But much less is said about making amends to or even asking forgiveness from yourself. Self-forgiveness is just as important to good recovery as making amends to others. However, it can be extraordinarily difficult.

Forgiving Yourself

Genuine self-forgiveness can help restore a person's sense that she has moral worth and dignity even if she has made significant mistakes and caused great harm to others or to herself. It all comes down to what she is willing to do in the present and future. She must acknowledge what she's done, repair as best she can and as circumstances allow, and commit to doing better in the future. The bitter irony is that the people who perhaps most need and deserve to forgive themselves cannot. The necessary reflection and acknowledgment can be very difficult because some people are burdened by forms of self-deception even as they come to more fully know and belong to themselves. Self-deception makes it difficult to identify when self-forgiveness is appropriate. While people may be reborn, regenerated, and rejuvenated, the old versions of themselves are never fully left behind. One consequence is that some people still struggle with less common forms of self-deception.

One particular form of self-deception is exceptionalism: A person holds herself accountable or blameworthy in ways that she would never hold others. She holds herself to a standard that is far higher than the one she uses for others. She may do this because she views her past transgressions as particularly egregious. This is a cousin to perfectionism. A person expects herself to be perfect and anything less than perfection is abject failure. She believes she controls the outcomes of all her actions. If those actions go awry, it must be her fault.

There are others who extend the realm of their responsibility to just about everything. This is expansionism. A person significantly overestimates his zone of responsibility, thereby assuming responsibility for acts and situations that are not his. If he sees himself as responsible for everything, he will always encounter failures and mistakes. Someone else may be the one making the mistakes, but he will still see himself as bearing responsibility. Perhaps he should have been the one to act or should have known someone else would mess up. Whatever the mistake is, he will always find a way to make it be about himself.

Expansionism's partner in crime is confirmation bias. Part of the reason he will always encounter his mistakes and failures is because he will actively look to see them. Every act confirms his inadequacy or culpability, which exacerbates shame. He believes that so many things he does are bad/wrong/hurtful, and this reinforces his view that someone *like him* doesn't deserve forgiveness.

These forms of self-deception are notoriously difficult to identify and interrupt because they are so familiar. More accurately, they are normal to those who operate under them; they mediate how people see themselves and others. This has very real consequences. Imagine a person who believes everything bad that happens in a relationship is her fault because of her drinking and drug use. Her partner may reinforce this belief along with the companion one that he has no responsibility. She takes his blame and combines it with her own. This may make a relationship go from bad to toxic to dangerous. She may realize after being sober for a period that she needs to leave her partner. The relationship is not good for her; it is actively harming her.

She feels as if she has really let herself down by staying for so long. She's wasted too many years with someone who not only didn't make her a better person but tore her down. She lost herself in alcohol and drugs. Why is self-forgiveness appropriate and what might it look like for her? Self-forgiveness is appropriate because it is a way to restore dignity, which is often damaged in toxic relationships. Self-forgiveness is a key step in rebuilding—or building for the first time—the sense that a person matters.

What might the acknowledgement, repair, and commitment that are crucial for self-forgiveness look like for her? She needs to explore her reasons for drinking and using drugs. Was she avoiding? Trying to cope? Something else? She also needs to acknowledge the history of the relationship and what patterns developed anew or continued from past relationships. She needs to acknowledge her feelings and reasons for staying, along with her reasons for leaving. Most importantly, she needs to acknowledge what was beyond her control, including her partner's responsibilities. This is a very hard thing to do.

The repair work takes several forms. To repair is to restore, rejuvenate, heal, and redeem one's self. One important step is to reframe. She may have a tape running through her head that she did all of this to herself; she chose to drink and she chose to stay for so long. She sees her harms as self-inflicted. If she were to reframe particular decisions, that may help to reframe the broader picture. For example, she may come to see that she had very few options—and each of them bad—to choose between. A rock and a hard place are both options, but neither is a good one. She may reframe her actions in light of those choices and realize she did the best she could in difficult circumstances. In fact, she may see she was rather clever in coming up with third options in many situations. Something like this may help her to see herself as having a little more worth than she had thought. This can be a huge achievement in healing and redeeming a sense of worth.

The commitment to a better present and future self builds upon the acknowledgement and repair work. The commitment to being a better person in the future must involve the commitment to treat yourself better by valuing and respecting yourself. It is a commitment to break old patterns of self-deprecation and self-denigration that aid and abet self-deception. When a person does this, she is less likely to tolerate others defining her value and worth for her. She may come to have more confidence in her choices, goals, hopes, and, most crucially, herself. This confidence is well-grounded; it is a confidence informed by humility. It is also uplifting and liberating, enabling her to better navigate life in recovery.

Stability in Recovery

Life in recovery is easier in many ways because alcohol, drugs, and other addictive behaviors are not contributing to the madness. They are no longer a person's habitual center of personal energy. The self-knowledge we acquire and the self-forgiveness we can give ourselves make us nimbler and more flexible, which in turn makes us better able to respond to the challenges we will face living in recovery. Flexibility is a virtue in recovery but so too is some degree of rigidity. Together, flexibility and rigidity provide stability. Too much of either may lead to problems. We need stability and flexibility to traverse difficult terrain in much the same way we may need a bridge to cross a divide. The bridge that best exemplifies the relationship between flexibility and rigidity is the eastern span of San

Francisco-Oakland Bay Bridge. James would like this comparison, I believe, since he was in San Francisco in 1906 and was shaken from his bed by a 7.9 earthquake. To be a reliable and useful bridge, it must be responsive to the needs and goals of the people who use it, as well as respectful of physical constraints. It must be constructed to withstand both the wear and tear of everyday use and a major earthquake. The bridge's proximity to two very large faults capable of producing significant earthquakes is one of the most salient considerations for its design and construction.

This self-anchored suspension bridge has only one tower, which is located closer to one side. The tower and deck are designed to move independently of each other, which is crucial in the event of an earthquake. The bridge is constructed to be able to sway. There are also piles driven deep into the water at angles to increase stability. Interestingly, the stability of this bridge isn't a matter of being able to resist movement, but rather being flexible enough to withstand the movement that would happen during an earthquake. The bridge is designed to move with an earthquake and not against it. This motion increases the likelihood of its survival.

Stability through flexibility is a crucial aspect of good recovery, and I would argue, any good life. Good recovery is designed to be responsive to the goals and needs of a person and to be respectful of physical, social, spiritual considerations and constraints. It may at first seem strange to think one must have a design for recovery, but good recovery requires intention and planning. It does not happen by accident or happenstance. One starts to generate reasonable goals that can be met. The goals may seem really small at first, but setting goals and meeting them requires hard work. At some point, a person will be able to set bigger goals for herself about what kind of person she wants to be and how she wants to show up in the world.

Recognizing needs is crucial but often easier said than done. Here too, hard work and practice are necessary since failing to identify needs produces a design that is not useful. The nature of addiction makes the needs very hard to identify and/or prioritize. Addictions affect a person physically, psychologically, and spiritually so each of these dimensions will produce needs. The needs may be in competition. Consider a person who has an opioid addiction. Psychologically, she may need to be free of all drugs, yet the use of suboxone could help to alleviate the physical cravings. Which need is more important? How might she come to a good decision about how to treat her addiction? Furthermore, a person with multiple addictions may have different needs for treating each addiction. One may be willing to go cold turkey on alcohol but will need nicotine patches for her smoking addiction.

Instead of looking to make a person's recovery fit a particular program, we need to make programs that fit our differing needs. Some programs will be better for an individual than others. Someone who has a strong Christian faith might feel immediately comfortable with Alcoholics Anonymous, while people from other faith traditions might need to stretch the concept of God to feel included. This book argues for a much broader conception of a higher and friendly power that includes anything bigger than our own small selves. Others who have left a faith tradition or do not come from one may find secular groups more inviting. Still other addicts will find groups using a cognitive behavioral approach to addiction and recovery more conducive to their needs. Some addicts will be opposed to any sort of group activity, and might pursue more solo therapy ventures or alternative practices. Some will quit cold turkey and never talk about it.

As James argues, our selves are always in process. Our material, social, and spiritual selves constantly change. We see changes in others and ourselves as we dry out, sober up, and start to live a life of sobriety. These changes can be significant. Recovery must remain responsive to these changes. If not, then one may be seeking stability in rigidity. Maintaining flexibility requires assessing needs and goals and looking at the means and methods for living soberly. Some people might to start to find AA confining; others who have tended to be more solo fliers might start to want the company of others in recovery. Some may finally try acamprosate calcium (Campral) to help with the withdrawal symptoms when stopping drinking, while others take naltrexone to block the high that comes from drinking.

Each of us will experience earthquakes in our own lives. If our stability is founded on flexibility rather than resistance, we have a better chance of weathering those earthquakes. Weathering the earthquakes doesn't mean avoiding damage. We will have the resources for recovering from and repairing that damage. One important reason we are able to do this is that we can meet the world with gratitude rather than grievance.

Gratitude over Grievance

Gratitude and not grievance becomes the habitual center of personal energy for people living with the acute fever. Gratitude and grievance are living attitudes with which we meet the world. People who live on the sunnier side of their misery threshold tend to greet the world with gratitude while those on the darker side meet it with grievance. James notes that even though we are reborn and regenerated after a conversion, some dimensions or traits of our old selves remain in some form. If we had been people who inclined more toward grievance and a sense of having been wronged when we were still using, we may still incline in that direction. The good news is that we may learn how to not clutch those grievances so tightly for so long.

Gratitude and grievance are not just emotions. Nor are they passing moods. Rather, gratitude and grievance guide attention and interest; they set the terms for how people see and meet the world. Gratitude and grievance play an important role in setting expectations and for assessing how well those expectations have been met. Gratitude and grievance become ways of living.

Grateful people see plenitude where others might see scarcity. While realities and actualities present challenges, they also present opportunities. Some of those opportunities may be unwanted, but there they are. A person may be grateful for an opportunity even if it doesn't pan out for her in the way she hoped. She may also be grateful for the opportunity to reach for something she had never before considered. Operating from gratitude may enable a person to take some risks in the knowledge that she may not get what she wants. She may have confidence in herself that she'll be okay with whatever happens. In the process, she may gain good experience that will serve her well later and help her to achieve new goals. Gratitude enables a person to be more willing to live on possibilities and maybes and take action where the results are uncertified. Gratitude expands a person's world, making it possible to have contact with that something More or something Bigger.

A world-view based on gratitude also helps a person to stay right-sized. Grateful people recognize how others have assisted them over the years. Whatever successes they have, they acknowledge that other people played important roles in those successes. This isn't to deny or minimize their own hard work but rather to situate that work in a broader context. Perhaps a stranger showed them kindness or a teacher spent extra hours tutoring or a boss worked out a more flexible schedule. Another may have been supportive in early days of recovery. When someone is able to acknowledge the help of others, this guards against an arrogance claiming everything she has is a consequence of only her own hard work. This is genuine humility, which is part of what it means to be right-sized. A grateful person recognizes that she's now in a position to help others in the ways she herself had needed. This is the other way of being right-sized. Being right-sized in both these ways further expands the world of those who meet life with gratitude. They will say Yes to life.

Someone who operates from grievance will see scarcity where others see abundance. The possibility of disappointment is always front and center in his decision making; it carries far more weight than the possibility of a good outcome. Grievance-based people become risk averse; they tend to stick with what they know even if it is not all that desirable because something different could be much worse. This is one way that grievance causes a person's world to contract.

Grievance-centered people also have a problem with being right-sized. If a person genuinely believes everything he has accomplished is solely his own doing and that he's achieved so much despite unfair treatment, he will over-estimate himself. He has difficulty seeing that others have helped him because most of his interactions with others are interpreted through a filter of offense or grievance. He sees himself as always being in a disadvantaged position relative to others. This sense of being disadvantaged means he will have a difficult time identifying situations where he has advantages and could help others. A person's inability to be right-sized contributes to the contraction of their world.

While not explicitly about gratitude and grievance, being sight-sized, or expanding and contracting a world, the Stoic philosopher Epictetus (50-135 AD/CE), whom

James quotes in *Varieties*, offers a powerful recommendation of how one ought to meet and respond to the world.
He says,

> Remember that you must behave as at a ban-
> quet. Is anything brought round to you? Put out
> your hand and take a moderate share. Does it
> pass by you? Do not stop it. Is it not yet come?
> Do not yearn in desire toward it, but wait till it
> reaches you. So with regard to children, wife,
> office, riches; and you will some time or other
> be worthy to feast with the gods.[29]

Don't be a person who watches how much others take from
the platter and gets mad in advance that it will be gone
by the time it reaches you. You won't enjoy the delights
already on your plate. In other words, don't lose the present by hording past grievances and cultivating future ones.
The person with gratitude appreciates what is on her plate
and that others are experiencing delight too. Living with
an acute fever is saying Yes to what you presently have,
and thereby opening new possibilities. As James notes,
"Magnanimities once impossible are now easy; paltry
conventionalities and mean incentives once tyrannical
hold no sway. The stone wall inside of him has fallen, the
hardness in his heart has broken down" (208). The stone
wall falls, the hardness softens, and each of us may find a
Heaven within.

William James's Own Over-beliefs

William James presented his Gifford Lecture series over the course of several days. These lectures became *The Varieties of Religious Experience*, which runs several hundred pages. Listeners and readers had to have some serious stamina, which was perhaps fueled by intense curiosity. No doubt many wondered about James's own beliefs. Throughout the lectures and text, he held those close to his chest. This he did in order not to prejudice or sway his listeners and readers.

Only at the very end of *Varieties* does James discuss his own over-beliefs about God, the More, and higher powers. It shouldn't be surprising that James had complex and complicated views about spirituality and religion. Some of his many social selves had conflicting stakes in the matter. As a son of Henry James, Sr., he inherited a distrust of established religions, a spiritual restlessness, and a disposition toward melancholy. It was William who read and edited most of his father's writings on spiritual matters. As an artist, he saw beauty that could elicit awe or horror. As a physician and a scientist, James had a profound appreciation of and respect for science's methodology and commitment to observation and verification. He was always concerned with well-formulated hypotheses that could be put to the test. As a philosopher, James was deeply suspicious of scholastic proofs of God's existence and nature. While our own human rational capacities may be awe-inspiring, they will never be up to the task of fully describing the universe and solving its riddles. Our rational capacity isn't always up to the task of daily living. As a highly educated man in cultures that were dominated by various forms of Christianity, James had more than a passing familiarity with that tradition's language, symbols, and theologies. As the one delivering the Gifford Lectures on natural theology, James knew his audience was comprised of highly educated Protestants Christians. These last two social selves of James help to explain his use of many examples invoking God.

James begins to tip his hand for all those readers and listeners who have reached his "Conclusions" lecture and chapter. There he reminds us that his primary task has never been to prove the truth of one religion over another. James turns to the paragon of healthy-mindedness and optimism, Walt Whitman, who not only wrote about but lived with an expansive impulse to move forward not knowing the destination or whether defeat or victory awaited there. This attitude prompts James to claim that our religious or spiritual impulses spring from "A sense of the exceedingness of the possible over the real" (383). This sense is what interests him and not theological questions such as: Does God exist? If so, what is his nature? How does he exist? These questions are irrelevant to his purposes.

James's task in *Varieties* has been to look for any commonality in the religious and spiritual experiences of people. He wants to explore what role these play in people's lives and how spiritual impulses add to life. In searching for any commonality, James offers a hypothesis that has two parts. The first is that there's a sense that something is wrong, missing, lacking, or not fully developed in us humans as we naturally stand. The second is that we are saved or transformed by making a connection to higher powers (384). Each person has both a higher and lower part of himself as he had discussed earlier in the context of the healthy-minded. That better part of each person may be just a tiny granule evading our awareness and consciousness. In coming to identify with and embrace the higher and better part, a person makes a connection to the something More. On behalf of all his readers and listeners, James asks in effect, "So what about that something More?" Is it just an idea or does it really exist? These sorts of questions and their answers, James says, are the stuff of our over-beliefs.

James the psychologist and scientist isn't willing to veer into answering these questions in ways that would go beyond the bounds of his present-day science. He takes himself and other psychologists to have shown there's more life in our total soul/mind than we're consciously aware. His comments here hearken back to his discussion of conversions. Incursions from the subconscious feel as if they come from a source that is not only external but higher. James's working hypothesis is that it is the higher faculties of our own minds acting and controlling. We experience a sense of union with this higher or More because our conscious and subconscious are connecting and expanding. This is why James says the conscious person is continuous with a wider self through which saving experiences come. He makes the radical claim that the world of our present consciousness is but one of many, any of which may have meaning for our life. While these worlds are mostly discrete and separate, they can become continuous at certain points where the higher energies filter in (392).

The connections to wider selves or something More produce both ideas and actions. Those who make these connections become regenerated or reborn; they become new people. All of *Varieties* has been focused on individuals who live religion or spirituality. Theology tends to abstractions, ideals, proofs, and principles. Religious impulses tend to actions. Our connections to a higher power or something More produce actions that make a new reality. Anything that is able to produce results is real, James claims. So what do we call this reality? Christians call it God, so James does too. James makes the bold claim that our connections to what he has called God may make God "more effectively faithful to his greater tasks" (393). This view that contact with God may somehow benefit God is not within the over-beliefs of typical Christians.

Perhaps invoking God and all the over-beliefs surrounding that term gave James pause. In "Postscript," James pulls back on that claim. He cannot accept popular Christianity nor can he accept scholastic theism. He worries that he has a streak of supernaturalism running through him. At the same time he disbelieves and cannot accept an Infinite All Powerful interventionist God having certain traits. He understands for many people that a union with something larger than our own selves will be taken as proof for God. That union, he says, may bring us peace. However, he baldly claims, all the feelings of that union are not proof of God's existence or nature. There's no support for the existence of an infinite God. That need for connection and union is powerful and part of our human nature. It is simultaneously a spiritual and practical need that can be met with the belief

> that beyond each man and in a fashion continuous with him there exists a larger power which is friendly to him and his ideals. All that the facts require is that the power should be both other and larger than our conscious selves. Anything larger will do, if only it be large enough to trust for the next step. It need not be infinite, it need not be solitary. It might conceivably even be only a larger and more godlike self...and the universe might conceivably be a collection of such selves, of different degrees of inclusiveness, with no absolute unity realized it in at all (397-398).

James notes that his position entails a polytheism that he does not defend at the end of *Varieties*. He takes this up explicitly later in *Pragmatism* (1907) and *A Pluralistic Universe* (1909). His polytheism of different realities or consciousnesses makes him suspect to Christians. James admits that he would never be able to please everyone. To Christians, he was too pantheistic or polytheistic with his claims of multiple realities and consciousnesses. To non-Christians, he sounded too much like a Christian with his God language. James knew the power of over-beliefs; they are frameworks for making sense of experience. Over-beliefs provide union, security, and guides for living. This is why people hold so tightly and pledge allegiance to them. People take their over-beliefs as proof of the truth or rightness of their particular religion. Dogmatism breeds intolerance, which entails certain perspectives will be ignored, neglected, or forcibly erased. Intolerance is a barrier both to learning and to acting morally. James offers a recommendation that we should treat the over-beliefs of others with tenderness and tolerance so long as they are not themselves intolerant (389). By bracketing his own until the very end of his lectures and gently reminding his listeners and readers throughout to do the same, James was living that commitment to tolerance. His hope was that his listeners would do the same.

In *Pragmatism*, James argues that the world is various and pluralistic as opposed to absolute and unitary. Put differently, the fabric of the universe is multi-colored and multi-textured. James continues to note that his task is not to offer a particular theology. Neither James as an individual nor pragmatism as a method of philosophy is atheistic. He reminds his readers that in *Varieties*, rather than eliminate God from the universe, he made room for the reality of God. This God may be one feature of many in the universe. He quickly follows this claim with one of the clearest statements of his own over-beliefs:

> I firmly disbelieve, myself, that our human experience is the highest form of experience extant in the universe. I believe rather that we stand in much the same relation to the whole of the universe as our canine and feline pets do to the whole of human life. They inhabit our drawing-rooms and libraries. They take part in scenes of whose significance they have no inkling. They are merely tangent to curves of history the beginnings and ends and forms of which pass wholly beyond their ken. So we are tangents to the wider life of things.[30]

The ideals of dogs and cats do, at times, overlap with human ideals. We and they all want food, water, rest, play, and love.

James continues to explore the questions about the nature of the More in *A Pluralistic Universe*. There, too, he hopes that religious experiences of the sort he so carefully assembled in *Varieties* will point toward the continuity of our consciousness with a wider one, whatever we may call it. Our interactions with our own consciousness and its parts, with each other, with dogs and cats, and with the wider spiritual consciousness expand that wider consciousness. We forge a union with it. For James, these religious experiences suggest that our natural experiences and our moral ones constitute only a fragment of human experience. A person having religious experience, James claims, is "continuous, to his own consciousness, at any rate, with a wider self from which saving experiences may flow in."[31] The evidence will pull us toward a belief in some form of superhuman life with which we may be co-conscious. Our becoming conscious of this wider life affects it as much as that connection affects us. This echoes what he said earlier in *Varieties* about making God more faithful to his own tasks.

For James, a life of religion or spirituality is not about theology but about experience. James was content to be a tangent to the wider life of things, willing to live on possibilities and embracing the maybes of life.

Our lives in recovery are about experiences as well. We become able to transform hard, painful, and even shameful experiences into meaningful ones. These experiences have helped to shape our material, social, and spiritual selves. We see so many possibilities where before we may have seen only inevitabilities. In reaching out to a something More, creating a Heaven within, and giving ourselves willingly to an expansiveness, we come to say Yes to all that life offers, both good and bad.

Appendix II

William James and
Alcoholics Anonymous

This book has charted the most significant divergence by Bill Wilson and Alcoholics Anonymous (AA) from William James. James's conception of higher power is far more open, inclusive, and expansive than what one finds in AA's 12 Steps. The language of the Steps changes substantially from Steps 2 to 3. Step 2 is "came to believe a Power greater than ourselves could restore us to sanity." In Step 3, that Power is identified with God to whom we decide to turn over our wills and our lives. Bill Wilson added the qualifier, "God as we understood Him." In Step 5, we admit to God the nature and extent of our wrongs in a quasi-confessional mode. Step 6 signals our readiness to have God remove our defects of character. Step 7 asks God to remove our shortcomings, while Step 11 recommends we seek through prayer and meditation to improve our conscious contact with God (as we understood Him). We are to pray only "for the knowledge of His will for us and the power to carry that out." The God of AA is a Christian God; it is a providential God who has dominion over us. This type of God does things to or for us while also having a plan for us. Our human agency consists in figuring out that plan and acting appropriately on the basis of it.

This God of AA is very much a consequence of Bill Wilson's over-beliefs. James would regard this as a form of crass supernaturalism. In many ways, Bill Wilson failed to heed James's warnings to listeners and readers of *Varieties* to bracket their own over-beliefs. Not doing so, James says, tends to impose uniformity over plurality. It is difficult for alternative views of a higher power to gain purchase within the program of AA. While individuals may be able to conceive or generate alternative conceptions, it requires an enormous amount of energy to do so. Maintaining and defending those views especially in early sobriety is a burden. To feel as if one's spiritual beliefs are less valid, not tolerated, and under dispute is a serious hindrance to sobriety. Had Bill Wilson heeded the suggestions of Hank Parkhurst, one of the earliest members of AA, about the "God language," AA would have been more inclusive, thereby offering help to a greater number of struggling people.

Bill Wilson appears to have experienced a sudden conversion in the Charles B. Towns Hospital in 1934. That experience changed his life; one of its practical fruits was that Wilson began to work with others struggling with alcohol. Among those with whom he worked was Dr. Robert Smith, better known in the AA community as "Dr. Bob," and Hank Parkhurst. These three—but mostly Wilson and Parkhurst—formed what became Alcoholics Anonymous. Bill Wilson was the primary architect of the 12 Steps and the primary author of *Alcoholics Anonymous* (1939), often referred to as The Big Book. Wilson's conversion is part of the founding—the mythology even—of AA. Wilson's experience became the basis for establishing a program of recovery.

Early in *Varieties*, James informs his listeners and readers that he is more interested in the spiritual experiences of individuals and far less in the religions founded on their basis. James expresses a worry that the spiritual experiences of one person can become the norm or measure for the experiences of others. This worry has very real concrete effect. Bill Wilson experienced a bright light and a big gust of spirit in his conversion. He immediately felt his desire to drink lifted. This was Wilson's experience; it worked for him. Many people who read The Big Book, especially the first 164 pages comprising the first edition, might think, "I've never had that sort of experience, so I really do not belong here." Others might offer, "I've had the bright lights and the big gust, but I still want to use more than ever." Only in the second printing of the first edition of The Big Book was an appendix added with the title "spiritual experience." In this important appendix, Bill Wilson recognizes that sudden conversions like his own are by no means the rule. Many people experience a more gradual transformation. This change, according to Wilson, is what William James would say belonged to the "educational variety." By this, he means gradual or voluntary. However, many people tend to focus on the original text and not this important appendix, which means the sudden conversion continues to function as the norm. For James, neither the origin nor the speed of the conversion is most important. The practical fruits of the spiritual tree matter most.

Bill Wilson in *Alcoholics Anonymous* makes it abundantly clear that the people most ready for a sudden conversion are those who, like him, had pretty much lost it all. People who have complete ego deflation are at rock bottom, which is where a person needs to land in order to make a dramatic change. This view is not only wrong but dangerous. The concept of rock bottom combined with its accompanying state of ego deflation makes it seem as if there is some objectively measurable point one must hit. A person could justify his continued use by still having more to lose. He could tell himself, "I am not there yet, so why bother," while minimizing what he has already lost. Here, too, uniformity is imposed over plurality and diversity. As James described, each person has their own misery threshold. What may be tolerable for one person is completely intolerable for another. Those who haven't lost it all or who haven't even lost that much may still want to change their lives and be willing to do things differently.

In the essay, "The Will to Believe," James explores situations in which a person must choose between two live or credible options, each of which carries momentous consequences. This is one way to understand the dilemma facing people who struggle with addiction. In such conditions, James argued that people have a right to hold beliefs where rational evidence falls short but where holding that belief helps to bring about the actuality of what is believed. This is one way to see faith as a working hypothesis. A person may do this; it is a matter of choice. In AA with its 12 Steps, that "may believe" turns more into a must believe in a particular set of over-beliefs. The gap between may and must is enormous and keeps an untold number of people from AA. For many, attending AA is not a live option because of the assumed role God plays. To enliven the hypothesis that AA has something to offer, there must be a much broader conception of a higher power.

One of the greatest strengths of Alcoholics Anonymous is people telling our own stories. Our stories help other people to make sense of themselves. We also become better able to make sense of ourselves. Each of us is an expert on his, her, or their own experience; we do not need to have specialists or professionals interpreting our stories' meanings and significance. There's a certain democratic flavor to AA that is shared with *Varieties*. James never adopted the stance of disinterested observer passing judgment on others. AA can function as an intellectual republic. There's no hierarchy in AA; there are no credentialed experts leading meetings, offering diagnoses, and providing counseling. The anonymity expectation has largely kept AA away from the investigating eyes of medicine, psychology, and sociology. It remains resistant to the drive to understand addiction primarily as a chronic brain disease. James would agree with many members of AA who see ourselves as addicted persons and not an addicted body part.

In AA, the newcomer and the old timer are equally important. The newcomers often remind people with longer term sobriety of what it is like to be caught in the grips of an active addiction or to have a tenuous grasp on sobriety. Newcomers help to keep it real in a sense for the old timers whose memories of the cravings, the suffering, and the chaos has dimmed. Newcomers provide important reminders of what might happen to anyone.

Those with longer term sobriety who have been "reaping the fruits of the spiritual tree," show what is possible for others whose habitual centers of personal energy shift away from actively using. Other people can help each of us see our higher or better self, James would say. Others show us our reflections in a plane mirror, as opposed to the convex or concave fun house mirrors we seem to use when looking at ourselves. Where one person cannot see her better self, another may be able to say, "I see her clearly." Each of us helps others not only to see but make a better or higher self.

The Promises of the Ninth Step echo James's description of the spiritual fruits, especially the ways life no longer is a drama of offense, drama, and repair. Where before a person careened, a rejuvenated or regenerated person can move around in the world with some confidence and equanimity. The internal strife and deep divisions are lessened, perhaps even healed. Warring selves declare peace. Bill Wilson wrote that we will know a new freedom and happiness. We'll be able to stand in proper relationship to the past. We will feel peace and serenity. Our self-pity and our selfish interests will transform into concern for others. We'll no longer feel useless because our experiences can benefit others. Our whole attitude and outlook on life will change. These things change, James claims, because we are no longer the same people. We become people who are more comfortable with possibilities and more willing to live on maybes. It is with and through other people that the Ninth Step Promises come true and we are able to reap the practical fruits of the spiritual tree.

Endnotes

1. Paul Fisher, *House of Wits: An Intimate Portrait of the James Family* (New York: Henry Holt, 2013), 69.
2. Ibid., 82.
3. Ibid., 83.
4. Ibid., 107.
5. Ibid., 108.
6. Robert D. Richardson, *William James: In the Maelstrom of American Modernis*m (New York: Mariner Books, 2001), 120.
7. Jane Maher, *Biography of Broken Fortunes: Wilkie and Bob, Brothers of William, Henry, and Alice James* (New York: Archon Books, 1986), 71-72.
8. Ibid., 73.
9. Ibid., 119.
10. Ibid., 128.
11. Ibid., 171.
12. Richardson, 375.
13. William James, "The Effects of Alcohol," in *The Works of William James: Electronic Edition.* Volume 19: Manuscript Lectures, 52.
14. American Psychiatric Association, *Diagnostic and Statistical Manual of Mental Disorders*, 5th edition (Arlington, VA: American Psychiatric Association 2013).
15. Ibid., 483-484.

16. Quoted in Robert D. Richardson, *William James: in the Maelstrom of American Modernism* (Boston: Houghton Mifflin 2007), 176.
17. Ibid., 120.
18. Ibid., 121.
19. This discussion of desire, wishing, and willing draws from James's *The Principles of Psychology*, chapter XXVI (New York: H. Holt and Company, 1890).
20. William James, *The Will to Believe and Other Essays in Popular Philosophy* (New York: Longmans 1896).
21. Ibid., 34.
22. Ibid., 54.
23. Ibid., 29.
24. Ibid., 54.
25. Ibid., 56.
26. Ibid., 33.
27. Homer, *The Odyssey*. Trans. A.T. Murray. (Cambridge, MA: Harvard University Press, 1995) Book XII, lines 185-190.
28. Michel de Montaigne, *The Complete Works of Michel de Montaigne* (London: Everyman's Press, 2003) 1280.
29. Epictetus, *Enchiridion* XV. Available at https://www.gutenberg.org/files/45109/45109-h/45109-h.htm. Retrieved 19 November 2019.
30. William James, *Pragmatism* in *The Works of William James: Electronic Edition*. Volume 1, 143-144.
31. William James, *A Pluralistic Universe* in *The Works of William James: Electronic Edition* Volume 4, 139.

Bibliography

American Psychiatric Association. *Diagnostic and Statistical Manual of Mental Disorders.* 5th ed. Arlington, VA: American Psychiatric Association, 2013.

Anonymous. *Alcoholics Anonymous Big Book.* 4th ed. New York, NY: Alcoholics Anonymous World Services, 2002.

Epictetus. *Enchiridion* XV. Available at https://www.gutenberg.org/files/45109/45109-h/45109-h.htm.

Fisher, Paul. *House of Wits: An Intimate Portrait of the James Family.* New York: Henry Holt, 2013.

Homer. *The Odyssey.* Trans. A.T. Murray. Cambridge, MA: Harvard University Press, 1995.

James, William. *The Principles of Psychology.* New York: H. Holt and Company, 1890.

———. "Is Life Worth Living," in *The Will to Believe and Other Essays in Popular Philosophy.* New York: Longmans, 1896.

———. "The Will to Believe," *The Will to Believe and Other Essays in Popular Philosophy.* New York: Longmans, 1896.

———. *The Varieties of Religious Experience.* Oxford: Oxford University Press, 2012.

———. "The Effects of Alcohol," in *The Works of William James: Electronic Edition.* Volume 19.

———. *Pragmatism* in *The Works of William James: Electronic Edition.* Volume 1.

———. *A Pluralistic Universe* in *The Works of William James: Electronic Edition,* Volume 4.

Maher, Jane. *Biography of Broken Fortunes: Wilkie and Bob, Brothers of William, Henry, and Alice James.* New York: Archon Books, 1986.

Montaigne, Michel. *The Complete Works of Michel de Montaigne.* London: Everyman's Press, 2003.

Richardson, Robert D. *William James: In the Maelstrom of American Modernism.* New York: Mariner Books, 2007.

Index

197